The Word Today

for mother,
with love
and gratitude

The Word Today

Reflections on the Readings of the
Revised Common Lectionary

Year C   Volume 1

Herbert O'Driscoll

Anglican Book Centre
Toronto, Canada

2001
Anglican Book Centre
600 Jarvis Street
Toronto, Ontario
M4Y 2J6

Cover illustration: Book of Hours, "Adoration of the Magi for Sext"

Canadian Cataloguing in Publication Data

O'Driscoll, Herbert, 1928-
  The word today : reflections on the readings of the revised common lectionary

Previously published under title: The word among us.
ISBN 1-55126-337-8 (Year C, v. 1)

1. Lenten sermons — Outlines, syllabi, etc. 2. Holy-Week sermons — Outlines, syllabi, etc. 3. Lent — Meditations. 4. Holy Week — Meditations. 5. Bible — Liturgical lessons, English. I. Title. II. Title: The Word among us.

BS511.5.O37 2001   251'.62   C00-933143-3

Contents

Using This Book

This book will provide reflections on the scripture passages of the Revised Common Lectionary from the first Sunday in Advent of Year C to the last Sunday after the Epiphany, now also called Transfiguration Sunday.

Each Sunday is offered in a simple sequence. There is a list of the Readings, then a short section called Weavings, in which I try to express an overall theme common to the scriptures of the day, as well as a sentence for each reading. This is followed by Reflections on the four passages in their traditional sequence of Old Testament reading, psalm, epistle, and gospel.

Some readers may have used a previous series called *Child of Peace: Lord of Life,* reflecting on the lectionary of the Canadian *Book of Alternative Services.* This second series, on another lectionary, is not a revision of the former. In writing this new series I have deliberately set aside the former books and have not referred to them in any way. Naturally, in some passages of scripture, the central theme will dominate any efforts a homilist may make to vary his or her interpretation.

These pages are not ready-made homilies. They respect the fact that scripture, the homily formed from it, the homilist him or herself, and the congregation, together form a living entity in which wonderful things can happen.

Most of the content offered here comes from nearly four decades of parish ministry. As I write, I am constantly aware that I am present with a sister or brother in ministry, ordained or lay, who is trying to say something to their people that will give grace and encouragement and vision and hope for the busy days that follow each Sunday. My hope is that these reflections will open some doors, and will assist in making many homilies that will eventually turn out to be very different from these notes. With this book go my prayers and best wishes for your part in the ministry of our Lord in which we both share.

Herbert O'Driscoll

First Sunday in Advent

Jeremiah 33:14–16
Psalm 25:1–9
1 Thessalonians 3:9–13
Luke 21:25–36

Weavings

The central theme of all these scriptures is encouragement. All through the texts, someone is either giving encouragement or seeking it.

First Reading. Jeremiah tells his contemporaries that, in spite of all evidence to the contrary, God will fulfil the promises made to his people.

The Psalm. The psalmist's ability to persevere, no matter what, springs from his conviction that God can be trusted. This becomes the source of courage in his life.

Second Reading. How pleasant it is to get a letter that makes it very obvious that the writer thinks highly of us. We hear this in Paul's letter to the community at Thessalonica. To read it aloud must have made the morale of that small community soar!

The Gospel. Our Lord wishes those who follow him to face the future with courage and strength. In the midst of turmoil some things will stand firm, some people will succeed in keeping their heads high. These are the images our Lord uses to describe the stance he hopes we may be able to achieve in the face of whatever happens.

Reflections

First Reading

It is worth noting that Jeremiah is writing from temporary imprisonment (33:1). Think of how much we owe to Christian voices who have written in and from prison. We think immediately of people like John Bunyan, who gave us *Pilgrim's Progress*, or Dietrich Bonhoeffer in this century, who gave us letters that are now spiritual classics. Teilhard de Chardin was in prison for a time, as was Charles Colson. The list is much longer. In every case, some kind of power seems to flow from those cells. Power certainly flows from Jeremiah in this passage.

"I will fulfil the promise," says the Lord. This is what Jeremiah's hope is based on. It is not just that he himself has done some analysis of the many factors that may affect the future. Being a very thoughtful and intelligent man, he undoubtedly had. But the basis for his confidence is his conviction that God can be trusted. Jeremiah would agree with Albert Einstein when the latter said, "God does not play dice!"

A righteous branch [will] spring up for David. This hope for the future is very much rooted in mundane reality. No squadrons of angels is being summoned. Instead, there will be a *person* who embodies hope for the future. God does work through men and women. Admittedly all are not great, nor do all exercise tremendous leadership or make highly significant contributions. Nevertheless, God works through humanity, using human gifts, sometimes transforming human failure.

He shall execute justice and righteousness in the land. This is how the action of God in history is always known. It will always show itself wherever justice is done. There is a lovely chant from the life of the Taizé Community. It sings again and again, *"Ubi caritas, deus ibi est"* (Where love is, God is). This is a deep and timeless truth. The Christian understanding of loving is very focused and realistic. To show the love of God, to be an agent of the love of God, goes far beyond our personal giving and receiving of love. We are asked to love justice, to long that it be done in all levels of human dealing. It is significant that, when we baptize a child, we turn to the whole congregation who has just reaffirmed the baptismal faith, and we ask, "Will you strive for justice and for peace among all people?" We ask this because we can always be certain that, wherever justice is done, there God is present.

Jerusalem ... will be called: "The Lord is our righteousness." Jeremiah is holding out the vision of a society whose life would reflect God's own goodness, such that its very name would be synonymous with the name of God! We may feel tempted to think that such a vision is utterly impractical and could never be fulfilled in time and history. The best we can do is to try to form pathetic approximations of such a society. But the important thing is that the call to such a society never leaves us, and the call to work for such a society resounds in our lives.

The Psalm

To you, O Lord, I lift up my soul ... I put my trust in you. Even the very first line of the psalm has an echo of Jeremiah's situation. The psalmist wants to lift himself out of the prison of his own self into the presence of God. But as soon as that break for freedom succeeds, we realize that life cannot be lived merely on a basis of trusting ourselves, however rich our own strengths and gifts may be.

Show me your ways, O Lord ... your paths. Our culture speaks incessantly about the journey of the self. The voice of Frank Sinatra croons a song about living life "my way," doing it "my way"! Notice how far beyond this shallowness the psalmist goes. Beyond my ways are the ways of God. Beyond my paths stretch the paths of God. They call me beyond the destinations of the self.

God teaches sinners in God's way ... God guides the humble. The human journey seen in the Bible is not a solitary journey, where the self can so easily become the sole reference and guide. The human journey we are shown is taken in companionship with God. When we look back, we see two sets of footprints!

Second Reading

How can we thank God enough for ... the joy that we feel before our God because of you. There is nothing quite as exciting and as pleasurable as being affirmed by someone else. One of the lovely things we see again and again in Paul's nature is his constant and ready affirmation of people. He affirms even when there are tough things to be discussed, even when some discipline has to be applied. It is easy to forget that this is precisely what God has done for our humanity, by coming among us in human form. God has affirmed us in the most powerful way possible! Paul wants more than anything to see the people in Thessalonica "face to face." Yet is not this what God has done in our Lord Jesus Christ? God has decided to come among us — to see us, and be seen by us, face to face!

Paul now expresses a longing that three things may happen in the Thessalonian community, and in any Christian community. *May our God ... and our Lord Jesus direct our way to you.* He has left them, and he wants to get back to them at some time. We might consider turning Paul's thoughts into a prayer for all those who, for any reason, have left our particular community. Are there ways in which some can be won back?

May the Lord make you increase and abound in love for one another and for all. Paul hopes that the life of the community will be rich in relationships within itself, and also that it will reach out in love beyond itself.

May [our Lord] so strengthen your hearts in holiness. In other words, may the members of this, or any other, Christian community clearly recognize that we are called to holiness. We can think of holiness as a kind of journey, not merely as a state that some people are in and others are not. Perhaps a simple way of expressing this is to say that holiness — ultimate holiness — is the nature of God. This is the destination to which we are called to journey.

The Gospel

Whenever we read a passage of scripture, we have company. It is not always company that we can see. As we listen to our Lord talking to the disciples, we hear the passage through their ears. Years later, when Luke published (to use our term) his book, people read it again, and it had echoes for their own time. Now we read this passage, and it speaks to us. Because its language and its images are so powerful, it speaks to us on many levels. We choose one.

Signs in the sun, the moon, and the stars. For us, as the century changes, there are many such signs — signs of our changing relationship with the surrounding universe. Even as I write, we have just placed a new lens system in the great eye of the Hubble telescope, which enables us to look out almost to the known birth time of the universe. We are preparing to reach out to touch the planet Mars. The tiny artifact called Voyager One is by now somewhere among the stars, crossing the infinite seas of our own galaxy. Is God calling us to a vocation among the stars? Is the human story only beginning? Signs put questions to us. Questions call us to consider who and what we are as a part of God's creation.

On the earth distress among nations. Perhaps there will always be dis-stress among nations — the stress of conflicting systems, conflicting visions of the individual and of society, conflicting needs for resources. Yet this will be particularly true in a time of great transition, such as we live in. It was true on the smaller world stage of our Lord's lifetime. It certainly became true for Christians in the fourth and fifth centuries, as the world of the empire began to disintegrate. For us the struggle between nations is becoming primarily economic, a struggle that brings distress to millions of lives in the most practical and immediate ways of poverty and unemployment.

Nations confused by the roaring of the sea and the waves. As we struggle to find ways for our swelling numbers to live in harmony with the earth, we can hear our Lord's words expressing the distress of the created order around us. Perhaps, more than anything else, we fear the ultimate pollution of the oceans around us. They cleanse the planet. Without them, life ends. Already they are protesting. There are signs that human actions are testing the capacity of the seas to fulfil their role in creation.

People will faint from fear and foreboding of what is coming upon the world. Attitudes to the future vary immensely. There are those who live quite unthinkingly and in utter selfishness. There are others who are deeply committed to lifestyles that contribute as far as possible to a more human future. But among many there is a deep fear of what is to come. Popular arts — especially films — are full of visions of a vastly overpopulated and totally urban world, where law has broken down and survival is a brutal struggle.

Then they will see "the Son of Man coming like a cloud." Here is an ideal example of a statement in scripture that speaks to us on many levels. We do not know what was in our Lord's mind when he spoke it. It is an image that he would have known since he was a child. It appears in the book of Daniel. As a Jew, our Lord would have been aware of the conviction among his people that a leader would eventually come to lead them from Roman oppression.

However, when our Lord speaks about signs in nature *(the fig and all the trees),* then referring to the coming of the kingdom of God, he seems to be talking about something far more significant than the fate of one people. *"Heaven and earth will pass away,"* he says.

The question is, How we are to apply his words to our own time? What does it mean to say that God comes in the flow of human events? Most certainly a Christian is committed to the belief that all of time and all of creation is within the rule of God, and will find its consummation and completion in God. How then does this hope form Christian attitudes and thinking?

The great significance of this passage for us lies in the attitude that our Lord calls for. *When these things begin to take place, stand up and raise your heads, because your redemption is drawing near.* Our Lord is saying something like this — if we truly believe that God is at the heart of human events, then we can experience life with confidence, knowing that all events have ultimate meaning and purpose within the mind and will of God.

To have such trust helps us to avoid the neurotic and self-destructive responses so common in contemporary society. Our Lord is speaking of these when he says, *"Be on guard so that your hearts are not weighed down with dissipation and drunkenness and the worries of this life."*

Second Sunday in Advent

Baruch 5:1–9
Canticle 19 (Luke 1:68–79)
Philippians 1:3–11
Luke 3:1–6

Weavings

In the scriptures today, we are being challenged to look beyond our self-imposed and limited horizons.

First Reading. We listen as Baruch reaches for the most lyrical language he can find to inspire the people of his time to look beyond the limitations they are facing.

The Canticle. Full of joy at the birth of his son John, Zechariah points those around him to the vistas of a long history in which the people of God have been preserved again and again from enemies and from danger.

Second Reading. Writing to the community in Philippi, Paul suggests that there are boundless possibilities ahead for their community because of the quality of their spirituality.

The Gospel. Pointing to a future of great change and challenge, John the Baptist electrifies his society by declaring that they must see God's hand in this process, and that they must respond.

Reflections

First Reading

In this passage, we hear the voice of someone who endured much in a grim chapter of history. Baruch was a loyal friend and follower of the great prophet Jeremiah. In Jeremiah's own book, we are told that Baruch and he went into exile to Egypt. Other sources say that Baruch was exiled in Babylon. The significant thing for us is the beauty and power of what Baruch says to his contemporaries. Some of this power comes from his echoing of the magnificent language and images of Isaiah (see Isa. 40, for example).

Take off the garment of your sorrow ... put on ... the beauty of the glory from God. There is something very easily missed here. Notice that the sorrow is ours but the glory we seek to exchange it for is God's. We are hearing something said to us repeatedly in the Bible, something that conflicts with much of today's thinking and advice. We read endless books about developing the self, training the self, nourishing the self. But the Bible calls us to do something more. It calls us to reach out for the self that is beyond our own self — the self of God.

Notice how the following verses sing a song of God. The name of God rings out again and again. *The robe ... that comes from God. God will show your splendour. God will give you ... the name — Righteous.* All of this is being sung to the city of Jerusalem. We read this passage and we hear this being said to our own society. Immediately we do so, we realize how very far Western society is from recognizing that the source of its life and energy is in God.

Arise O Jerusalem, stand upon the height ... see your children ... from west and east. In what sense are we called to a greater vision? It may be that we need to *stand upon a height* and look beyond our own struggling Christian experience, to where Christian faith is spreading and showing immense energy. We need to look to areas of Africa and Asia. We need to be aware of the immense sacrifices being paid for Christian faith, of the widespread martyrdom in our generation. We tend to think that dying for the faith ended when Christians ceased to be thrown to the lions in ancient Roman arenas. Nothing could be further from the truth!

God has ordered that every high mountain ... be made low ... and the valleys filled up, to make level ground. The word from God to us is that we will be given grace to scale the mountains of the many concerns that seem to loom over Western Christian life and Christian churches today, that the many valleys of anxiety and despair that are sometimes present in Christian experience will be *filled up.* With what ? With the joy with which God will lead, *in the light of his glory, with the mercy and righteousness that come from him.*

The Canticle (Zechariah's Song)

Let's remember where we are in this passage. We are sharing the celebration of a Jewish family, probably gathered as an extended family. We are celebrating the most wonderful of occasions — the birth of a child. But this child is totally unexpected and, therefore, all the more cause for joy! When Luke tells us that Zechariah was *filled with the Holy Spirit,* it is very likely that he not only sang but he danced!

Blessed be the Lord God ... he has raised up for us a mighty saviour. We can't help noticing a very real difference between ourselves in our culture and Zechariah in his. We would begin by speaking of the personal joy we have because of this birth. Then, perhaps, we would bring in the family, but it is likely that we would stop there. We might wonder aloud about what this newborn would eventually do in life, but this is as far as we would go. Zechariah, however, walks immediately on to the stage of the nation's life and celebrates God's action there. For him the individual, family, extended family, tribe, and nation are all a single organism. It is interesting that we are experiencing a longing to return from the highly developed individualism of our society, to recapture some sense of being linked to one another. There is a growing longing for greater neighbourliness. A new generation is showing signs of wishing to stay within reasonable reach of family so that children have a sense of their roots. All of this comes to us in biblical moments like Zechariah's song.

Through his holy prophets he promised of old. Another rich gift that we see Zechariah possessing is a sense of the long story of himself, his family, and his people. We are seeing an increasing longing for this awareness in our own culture. Sometimes, to our surprise, we look rather longingly at such an awareness being very much alive in the Native peoples in our midst. We so easily forget that our own sacred writings — the Bible — remind us of this need in ourselves and encourage us to recapture a sense of story and a sense of community.

You, my child, shall be called the prophet of the Most High ... to prepare his way. This was to prove true for John. His whole life was to point people towards Jesus. But we, too, can look at a child and express the same hope for him or her — that he or she may be the kind of man or woman who becomes a channel of God's working in all sorts of ways. My prayer for my child is that he or she will grow to live and to relate to others in such a way as to make opportunities for our Lord to enter into those lives and situations.

Second Reading

The reason that collections of letters can be so fascinating is that we really meet someone in their pages. Letters reveal us. They make clear how we are feeling at the time. Paul is no exception as he writes to the Christian community in Philippi. He is happy. Things there are going extremely well — unlike in some other communities to whom he has to write from time to time!

I thank my God ... constantly praying ... for all of you. I remember once seeing a large photograph of a congregation on a refrigerator door. They were all gathered as closely as possible in the area of the altar, all looking up at the distant camera. Individual faces were tiny — it was the group that was important. I remarked on this to a friend, who replied that he often offered a quick prayer for the whole Christian community. In our instinctive individualism, we tend to pray more often for particular people than for the community.

Your sharing in the gospel. It struck me that it would be hard to find a better definition of the business of a Christian congregation. When we preach, we share the gospel. That's obvious. But there are many other things we do. When we worship, we share the gospel. When we meet as committees, we need to remember that we share the gospel. The business of a synod is to share the gospel. The criteria by which we need to judge every aspect of a program that we design and implement is whether it will share the gospel. Above and beyond and all around the most practical and mundane things of our church's life — such as finances, upkeep of buildings, paying taxes, and all the rest of it — we are nevertheless gathered to share the gospel.

This is my prayer, that your love may overflow more and more. Notice the implication here. The one thing a Christian community does not do is to rest on its oars, to become content with what it is at any given time. Notice too what is primary for Paul in the life of a congregation — the quality of its mutual love, the quality of mutual caring that is shown in its ongoing life.

That your love may overflow with knowledge and full insight. Paul seems to be saying that the task of loving needs to be thoughtful, sensitive, and insightful. There is no clumsy, over-emotional invading of people's lives. There is careful assessment of their need, knowledge of their personality, and thus some insight into how this particular person can best be shown love.

The Gospel

Tiberius the Emperor. Pontius Pilate the governor. Herod the ruler. Philip the ruler. Lysanius the ruler. Shakespeare often introduced a scene with the stage direction, "Trumpets and Alarums." Everyone would be jolted into paying attention. That's what Luke does here. He brings on a whole glittering procession of powerful personalities. His "camera" scans over Roman power, Jewish political power, not to mention priestly power. Then he presents us with a wonderful anticlimax. We look through his camera and we see the most extraordinary figure. He is the very antithesis of all the others. No fine clothes — instead, ghastly skins. No well-fed figure — instead, a body lean and tough, a face weathered by desert suns. Ironically, in spite of the great claims of all the others (the Emperor calls himself a god, and the High Priests claim to talk to God), it is to this extraordinary outsider that *the word of God came !* Apart from anything else here, this moment in scripture should alert us to the danger of assuming that God uses only this or that "official" channel — person, organization, tradition — to speak.

"Prepare the way of the Lord." The very first thing that John does is to push away any "camera" we might want to point at him. He tells us immediately that the whole point of his presence and his words and his work is to prepare for someone else. The more one thinks about it, the more one realizes that this is — or should be — equally true of everything we try to do in

congregations. Everything a church tries to say and do and organize is about someone else! It is about Jesus! Certainly, much of a congregation's life is about showing the kind of mutual love that Paul asks of the people in Philippi. But this love is carried out so that people may discover the love from which all love springs — the love of our Lord! In the same way, John points out that everything he says and does is for an objective beyond both himself and his hearers. Everything he does is so that *all flesh shall see the salvation of God.*

Third Sunday in Advent

Zephaniah 3:14–20
Canticle 3 (Isaiah 12:2–6)
Philippians 4:4–7
Luke 3:7–18

Weavings

All through these scriptures, spiritual help is being offered to lift the burden of fear and anxiety.

First Reading. The prophet Zephaniah has harshly condemned his society. He is convinced that a high price will have be paid by the whole nation. But, having said all this, he takes great care to point to the presence of God among them and the resulting spiritual resources available to them, if only they will claim these resources.

The Canticle. For Isaiah, fear and anxiety are lifted when there is utter trust in God. Because God has done great things in the past, great things can be expected.

Second Reading. The source of peace lies in God. The way to this peace is through prayer and in the joy of believing that God is all in all.

The Gospel. Even though John's manner is harsh, his words are received as good news. He is showing that a way into the future is possible if people are prepared to change their attitudes.

Reflections

First Reading

It is a worthwhile exercise to read through this beautiful and lyrical passage, and to realize how it achieves what it sets out to do. You realize that you are in the presence of a wise and gentle counsellor. This counsellor is not working with an individual, as we tend to assume, but is talking to a whole people. He knows that this people is anxious and fearful, and that they have cause to be. He believes that there is considerable trouble ahead, which is probably unavoidable. Wisely he begins to help his people concentrate, not merely on the future that must be endured, but on the possibilities that may exist beyond the trouble. He begins to speak about God and the relationship between God and this people. He points to seven important things that the people need to realize. They can be important for us as well.

Sing aloud ... shout ... rejoice and exult. The first thing the counsellor says is calculated to surprise, to jolt his listeners out of the grip of anxiety. He implies that there actually are some reasons for singing. Some congregations need to be reminded of this! There are at least six reasons for singing and rejoicing, in spite of all the pressing agenda many people feel.

The first reason for singing and rejoicing is that we and God are linked in a relationship. It is easy to miss this particular meaning in the phrase, *O daughter Jerusalem.* Christian faith is not information about some object we call God. It is a relationship with a living being we know as God.

The second reason for singing and rejoicing is that, in spite of the difficulty we have in believing it, we are always forgiven and accepted by God. *"The Lord,"* says the prophet to his people, *"has taken away his judgements against you."*

The third reason is that God is actually with us. *The Lord is in your midst.* In spite of the insistent assumption of our culture to the contrary, we are not alone. We are so familiar with statements like this that they have almost lost their power to reassure and strengthen. We need to practise the presence of God in small but powerful ways. As a discipline during the eucharist, we might always look up at the time of the breaking of the bread and deliberately ponder the mysterious fact that God is in the midst of us.

The fourth reason for rejoicing is that God has the power to renew us if we are prepared to be open to that power. *The Lord your God ... will renew you in his love.* Someone was saying recently that he would always remember the first time he came across the text of John 3:16 in Latin. It says, *"Deus delexit"* (God delighted in the world so much). For him it followed that, if God delights in the world, then God delights in each one of us who is part of that creation. The idea that God delights in me, in spite of all the reasons why I cannot always delight in myself, is immensely renewing.

The fifth reason for rejoicing is that I have an ally in my efforts to deal with the many things that oppress me as a very human being. God says, *"I will deal with all your oppressors."* In other words, God is assuring me that I am not alone in my struggles. In this particularly healing part of the passage, God promises not to forget *the lame ... and the outcast.* Hearing this on a personal level, I am being told that even those parts of me that are wounded and weak will know the grace of God. Even further, those things in me of which I am ashamed will be offered grace. *I will change their shame into praise.*

The sixth reason for song is that God can be grace to us in our efforts to bring the torn and fragmented parts of our lives together. This brokenness in us all of us can make us feel like exiles. We may seem exiled from our deepest self, from other people, from God. In this passage, God speaks to us perhaps some of the loveliest words we can hear: *I will bring you home.*

The Canticle

It is God who saves me; I will trust in him ... my stronghold ... my sure defence ... my Saviour. The stance of faith in Judaism is always outwards from the self to a reality beyond the self. This opening phrase implies that salvation, security, stability — whatever term we wish to use — is not found merely within the autonomous self. Rather, there is a deep relationship between the self and God, and it is from this relationship that strength is drawn.

You shall draw water with rejoicing from the springs of salvation. In biblical times someone had to go every day to the well for water. In the same way the self must go to God to refresh the spirit. Otherwise, the spirit dries up and eventually dies.

Give thanks to the Lord ... Sing the praises of the Lord. Another great realization of Judaism — one handed on to Christian faith — is that worship is intimately connected with the relationship between the human being and God. It is as if worship is to our relationship with God as lovemaking is to our relationships with each other. In each case, the relationship is nourished and enriched by what we offer to one another.

Second Reading

Rejoice in the Lord always; again I will say, Rejoice. Because we are often at our most personal when we write letters, our mood at the time of writing comes through clearly. Because Paul is writing to a community whose life has remained joyful and healthy, he conveys a feeling of celebration. There is joy in

Philippi; therefore, Paul feels joy. We experience the same thing when we come in contact with the life of a congregation, either as a visitor or a member. A healthy vitality, and a sense of the love and presence of our Lord being shared, can be wonderfully contagious.

Let your gentleness be known to everyone. There is a kind of wistfulness in this expressed hope of Paul. Certainly there were other communities — Corinth would have been one — where he wished he could find the quality he named as gentleness in Philippi. There are communities today that could do with this lovely text being emphasized in their congregational life! We need to remember this quality when we differ from one another in the ways that we understand and express Christian faith.

The Lord is near. It is possible to interpret this statement as a reminder of the expectation of the Lord's imminent return. It may also be possible to hear these words as referring to the qualities that Paul has just been naming in the congregation at Philippi. He has spoken so far of joy and gentleness. Is he suggesting that it is precisely in these qualities that the presence of our Lord is made possible?

Do not worry about anything. One can be facile in the use of this scripture. But we are so made that we cannot simply decide not to worry. Worry is an element in our human nature — admittedly more in some than in others, but to a degree in all of us. There is a truth here. Congregations can do a great deal of worrying. Will the money come in this year? Will we be able to get teachers for the children? Will the roof last another few years? All these concerns are legitimate. But the irony is that the answers to these and other such questions depend on a whole set of *other* questions. Is this a congregation whose life is essentially healthy? Is scripture a part of our lives, besides a few passages heard on Sunday? Is worship a living and vibrant experience? Is there mutual pastoral caring in evidence? Is anyone praying for others in the congregation? Is there outreach from the congregation into the surrounding community? While it may not reflect Paul's intention, we could risk adding a single small word to his statement, to give ourselves a salutary warning. Maybe we should remind ourselves not to worry about *just* anything! If we must do some worrying, let us worry about essentials!

In the next moment Paul suggests what some of these essentials are. *In everything by prayer and supplication with thanksgiving let your requests be made known to God.* It is perfectly legitimate for our prayer requests to reflect our worries. Paul is saying that, instead of merely harbouring our worries, we should place them right up front before God, as material for prayer! Then they cease to be worries, locked into the seething prison of our own minds and hearts. They become prayer requests openly expressed, honestly admitted! And what happens when we do this? Paul tells us, in words that shine from the pages of the new testament. *The peace of God, which surpasses all understanding, will guard your hearts and your minds in Christ Jesus.*

The Gospel

John said to the crowds that came out to be baptized by him. The crowds did indeed come down to the Jordan from Jerusalem. John did not go to them. This could have seemed the obvious thing for him to do. After all he was only one man, while they formed a large city. Why risk failure by staying in the Jordan valley away from the city? Perhaps because John realized that only if he could draw these people out of their familiar and busy streets would he get them to see the realities of their society and the need for great change.

The same can be true for us in congregational life. Sometimes it is essential for us to leave our familiar surroundings in order to reflect about the assumptions and habits of those surroundings. We need to look back from the outside at who we are, what we are doing, how we are doing things, and at the changes we need to consider.

Bear fruits worthy of repentance. We used the image of going outside our corporate situation in order to look back and see it in a new light. This can be just as necessary in our personal life. This is what John demanded of those people. By pausing to think about the two words *bear fruits,* we can capture an important element of repentance. Repentance is not merely turning back and looking and considering. Real repentance involves acting on what we see when we do turn and look back!

Do not begin to say to yourselves, "We have Abraham as our ancestor." John did not merely know his contemporaries. He knew human nature in any age! One of the defences we use against the need to change is our claim of the infallibility of tradition. This claim has power, because traditions are in themselves worthy and good. It is quite true that we should not smash traditions unthinkingly. But it is also true that God is a God of change as well as of changelessness. How do we tell when we need to respond to one or another of these realities?

The ax is lying at the root of the trees; every tree therefore that does not bear fruit is cut down and thrown into the fire. Here the criteria for change is very clear. We look at what is and we assess its performance. Why was this gift, this tradition, first given? Is it still able to produce what it once did? If not, is God demanding that we act — not merely to destroy the tradition but to renew it? This last question is very important.

The crowds asked [John], "What then should we do?" It is very obvious that there was something about John that communicated action. We need to see this clearly in our culture, because there is a temptation for us to think that, when we have discussed something, we have dealt with it! We often fall into this trap with public issues. We do a television special on this or that issue, and we believe that somehow it has been dealt with and we can now move on to the next issue! A congregation will discuss endlessly the desirability of this or that change — as will the church at other levels of its life — as if the mere thinking about the issue is to act about it. To those who heard John, something more was communicated. Group after group repeated the phrase, *What should we do?*

Who ever has two coats must share ... Collect no more than the amount prescribed for you ... Do not extort money ... by threats. The other admirable trait we see in John is the clear focus of his directives. There is no vague exhortation to something indefinable called "change." That kind of exhortation can be frustrating and self-defeating. For John there is always a specific change. It is always something that can be done by a personal decision. John would have been the first to agree with the prayer, "O Lord, change the world (or the church, or whatever large entity we have in mind), beginning with me!"

One who is more powerful than I is coming; I am not worthy to untie the thong of his sandals. Here is the magnificence of John as a human being — unflinchingly self-effacing, always pointing towards Jesus. Any leadership that is prepared to follow the same path will most likely see the same response. To emphasize again and again that beyond all the gifts within a congregation — gifts of clergy, lay leadership, the congregation in general — there stands the supreme gift of Jesus as Lord. This is to ensure spiritual health.

So, with many other exhortations, he proclaimed the good news to the people. In spite of the fact that he starts out by addressing the crowd as a generation of vipers! In spite of the fact that he rigorously probes their resistance to change. In spite of the fact that his specific replies are sharp and incisive, John's addresses are still heard as good news. Why? Because nothing is more relieving of fear and anxiety and indecision than presenting a course of action that is clear, focused and, above all, do-able!

Fourth Sunday in Advent

Micah 5:2–5a
Canticle 18 (Luke 1:47–55)
Hebrews 10:5–10
Luke 1:39–45 (46–55)

Weavings

The strong and beautiful song of all these scriptures can be stated in one word — birth.

First Reading. To a people feeling the frustration of being literally walled in by enemies comes the news that one is coming who will be able to move them beyond any walls.

The Canticle. A woman considers the child she is about to bring to birth. Her imagination soars until the whole world and the whole of history become the arena of her child's influence.

Second Reading. The writer stands in front of the area where temple sacrifice is offered, and he realizes that things will never be the same since Jesus offered himself as victim on the cross.

The Gospel. In the ecstatic encounter of two women, the coming birth is celebrated.

Reflections

First Reading

Walled around ... siege is laid against us ... with a rod they strike ... but ... The little word *but* can be used very powerfully. The writer — probably the original speaker — describes the present reality in pitiless and stark terms. His people are prisoners, under siege; their leadership is humbled, treated with contempt. Then comes the powerful *but* that will lead into the contrasting reality that he wants to show them. Before we look at this reality, it is worth noting a wonderful irony hidden in a phrase in the first verse of this reading.

With a rod they strike the ruler of Israel upon the cheek. Micah is of course referring to present enemies and their contemptuous treatment of the present unfortunate ruler. But we with Christian ears immediately recall another and very different kind of ruler who also was struck on the cheek and treated with contempt. And we know how our Lord triumphed over this, and over far worse treatment. We are being sent a message. To be weak does not mean that one is helpless. To be a prisoner does not mean that one will be a prisoner for ever. The fact that there are walls does not mean that they cannot be breached.

But you O Bethlehem ... one of the little clans ... shall come forth. We are hearing a repeated theme of scripture. It is from an unexpected source that a new thing comes. *When she who is in labour has brought forth.* It is from the unknown and unnamed and seemingly insignificant that the birth of the *new* comes.

The rest of his kindred shall return ... He shall stand and feed his flock ... They shall be secure. This new ruler will not merely preside over a situation where the main objective is survival in captivity. He will be in a position to draw people around him, to be a resource to them.

Let us now look at the preceding passages through the lens of our own situation as a Christian church. There is much that has today's church *walled around with a wall.* Many feel under siege. *But* — most wonderfully — there is absolutely no indication that our Lord is in any way walled in! Books about him pour off the presses. Arguments about his words and his work abound. According to David Tracy of Chicago, very few people realize that more has been said and written about Jesus Christ in the last two decades than in the whole preceding two millennia! In many parts of the world, millions are returning *as the rest of his kindred.* In this sense, our Lord is *great to the ends of the earth.* Much of the life of the church may feel a prisoner of the culture, and much of its energy may be directed to mere survival. *But* wherever there is a realization that our Lord is stunningly alive, a lot of institutional walls begin tumbling and there is a new sense of freedom and a new daring to explore unknown territory and to claim it for him.

The Canticle

My soul proclaims ... my spirit rejoices ... the Almighty has done great things for me. Nothing could be more deeply personal. This is a marvellous example of a legitimate sense of the self as a receiver and channel of grace from outside the self. Mary is deeply conscious of herself as a channel of God's grace and God's action. This does not mean that she understands what is taking place. All she knows is that something extraordinary is happening and that it will have consequences beyond her understanding.

This magnificent song, this Magnificat, as we call it, becomes powerful to the extent that each one of us can make it our own. We have grown up in a Christian tradition that abounds in such phrases as *the faith of the church* or *the faith once delivered to the saints*. And all of this is wonderful, as long as there comes a moment when we appropriate this faith to ourselves, when the faith becomes *my faith*. There has to be a moment when we sense that something of God is being born in us and we say, *"My soul proclaims the greatness of the Lord, my spirit rejoices."* To discover a personal faith like this is not to step away from what we mean by the faith of the church or the faith of the saints. The very opposite holds true. When we appropriate the grace of God to ourselves, we are then graced and released to truly become a living cell in the body of the church and a living servant in the community of the saints.

The fact of the matter is that we are all "Mary," each one of us potentially a human womb in which the eternal Christ wants to be born.

Second Reading

Sacrifices and offerings you have not desired, but a body you have prepared for me. In the thought of this unknown writer, we see Judaism, and the new Christian faith that has sprung from it, come to a parting of ways. For the first time we hear deep, probing questions about something taken for granted for centuries in Jewish worship — the regular sacrificial system of the Temple. This is not the first time it has been questioned. The prophets asked much the same thing centuries before. But these new Christians believe that, this time, an alternative has actually come, and that it will make the sacrificial system unnecessary.

Notice how the writer has our Lord actually speak as we overhear him. It is as if we are listening to our Lord as he ponders his mission. He is certain that something is missing in these sacrifices. *In burnt offerings ... you have taken no pleasure.* What is the alternative? Jesus realizes that the only alternative is complete and utter self-sacrifice. Then he declares himself prepared to be this person. *Then I said, "See, God, I have come to do your will."*

How does this passage speak to us personally? It echoes what we have heard already in these scriptures. When the writer has our Lord say, *"See, O God, I have come to do your will,"* we realize that this is exactly what each one of us at some moment must say of our own relationship with God. Who am I? I am someone who has come to do God's will. How did I become this? By nothing less than my baptism!

Look again at how the writer has our Lord consider the sacrificial system of his tradition and then come to a decision about his own role. In the same way, we need to consider the church as we know it, and while appreciating the gifts and graces it offers us, we need to realize that we must make a personal response to this tradition. In a sense, the church is incomplete without each one of us. This is not self-importance. It is a simple and wonderful fact. And when we realize it, we have made a tremendous breakthrough in our understanding of our baptism. It might be a good idea for every one of us in the congregation to take out this text and say out loud, *"See, God, I have come to do your will."* Thanks be to God!

The Gospel

If this gospel passage had background music, it would be soaring and glorious and joyful!

In those days Mary set out and went with haste to a Judean town. We don't know why she went. Perhaps Elizabeth was the one person who would understand the way that Mary's world had exploded. The point for us is that she went because she had to share her news. As she journeys, she calls every one of us to travel with her, to learn to share in some way the faith that is in us.

Most of us do not find this easy. We don't seem to realize what we could achieve by even the simplest actions. It is true today that so many people have slipped away from involvement in church life, yet have a longing for what they once valued. And it can be so simple to mention, in the company of friends, that you have discovered something you value in a particular worshipping community. That is sufficient. No long sermons, no great proclamations, just a simple reasonable statement that can sometimes have the most interesting consequences. Sometimes there may be somebody present whose heart beats a little faster because of the possibility of finding Christian community again. As with Elizabeth, a child of new-born faith may leap in that person's womb.

"Why has this happened to me?" cries Elizabeth. It's a cry we often utter in very different circumstances. Elizabeth asks it in a moment of joy. We usually ask it in a moment of suffering. If something wonderful happens to us — for instance, if we discover new faith kindled in us for reasons we don't know — and if we ask Elizabeth's question, we might realize that the gift has been given so that we may respond by acting in some important or special way.

There is something else in Elizabeth's words that we can appropriate to our own experience. Speaking to Mary, she says, *"Blessed is she who believed that there would be a fulfilment of what was spoken to her by the Lord."* Elizabeth seems to be suggesting that Mary has been blessed with this child because she assumed that the message of the angel would come true. The same needs to be true in our own soul's journey. We need to be a person who expects God's promises to come true.

Take a very simple example. When we kneel or stand to receive the food of eucharist, we are given not only sacred bread and wine, we are also given a promise of God. Sometimes that promise is expressed in a statement that tells us to "feed on him in your heart with thanksgiving." Another such statement can tell us that this food is "the bread of heaven." For the most part, these wonderful statements slide across our minds and are gone — if we are even aware of them. But we need to hear clearly and piercingly that we are being promised spiritual grace for our lives. This eating and drinking is essential to our soul, as the food we will enjoy after the service is essential to our bodies. The more we become conscious of such things, the greater their power to truly nourish. The more we believe them to be true, the more they grace us. As with Mary, the things of God come to birth within us.

Christmas Day

Isaiah 9:2–7
Psalm 96
Titus 2:11–14
Luke 2:1–14 (15–20)

Weavings

On this day we meet people who are conscious that God has acted to bring something into being, and they are trying to understand what the consequences are for themselves.

First Reading. Isaiah is leading his people in the celebration of a new king. Their hope is that oppression will be lifted by this new regime, that a new political reality is coming to birth, which will, among other things, bring peace.

The Psalm. Again a nation is being led in the celebration of some event that has given great joy and hope for the future. As always in the psalm, the glory is given to God for this event, whatever it may have been.

Second Reading. The writer sees himself and his contemporaries between two comings or showings of Christ as Lord. The past coming is in his birth; the future, in his return as Lord.

The Gospel. We are present at that moment when the mystery we call Incarnation enters into history.

Reflections

First Reading

It is remarkable how a change of political administration triggers hope for the future. In this passage, there is a new king. But same thing happens when a new president is elected in the United States — even when a president begins a second term — or a change of government takes place in Canada or any other country. There will be snide remarks and some cynicism, but even the cynic cannot avoid hoping, just a little, that some good things will happen.

In this situation there is great excitement. Biblical scholars say that it may be Hezekiah who has just become king. *Deep darkness* is about to give way to *light*. People exult. There is a feeling that things are going to be much better. They look at their new king and shout, *"The bar across [our] shoulders ... you have broken."* There is the fervent hope of peace, an ending to *the boots of the tramping warriors and all the garments rolled in blood.* Because we are in what we call today the Middle East, every expression of joy is exaggerated, which is normal in this culture. The new king is *Wonderful ... Mighty ... Everlasting Father, Prince of Peace.* There is not going to be just peace — it will be *endless peace.* There is not going to be just a period of righteousness and justice — it is going to last *forevermore.*

So why read this long-ago national outpouring of joy on Christmas Eve? For one thing, it has been linked with this time of Christmas joy for untold centuries, particularly because of the two lines telling us that a child has been born for us, a son given to us. The moment the words are said and the picture is in the mind, there comes the image of another child, another son. Our minds are transported — in more senses than one — to Mary and her child, to the giving of her son. The moment this happens, we begin to apply the things said about a long-ago ruler to this — what shall we say? — ruler. Then we realize that this is precisely what this child has become for us if we are Christian. He rules in our hearts if we believe him to be Lord.

If our Christian faith is a living and growing faith, deepening over the years, then we are saying that his *authority shall grow continually* within each of us. When we speak of a long-ago king bringing endless peace, we mean that knowing Christ as Lord can bring a sense of peace to our lives. When we hear a long-ago hope of righteousness, we realize that the same hope is within us, that we will be given the grace to live lives that will bring us into a right relationship with ourselves, with others, and with God. When we read of an ancient longing for justice, we hope that, because of our Christian commitment, we will feel called to act for justice in whatever ways we can.

The Psalm

We have only to say or sing the first verse, and we are caught up in the mood of this song. Every person around us is singing. Absolute confidence in God is everywhere. *Great is the Lord ... the majesty and magnificence of his presence!* All eyes look around the temple area and the shout goes up, *"Oh, the power and the splendour of his sanctuary!"*

How can we identify with this kind of ecstatic outburst? Perhaps by taking a moment to realize the wonder of what we are celebrating. Our problem is that wonder is sometimes crushed by familiarity. We are celebrating nothing less than the coming of God into time and history. Often these days we hear about UFOs. There is an endless public appetite for television stories of extra-terrestrial visitors. We have an insatiable curiosity for this kind of thing. But to be a Christian means that we believe that this planet has indeed been visited from beyond, that the unimaginable power of a creating God has entered the human story, even entered a human womb, making it the mysterious ship for that wondrous voyaging.

Second Reading

We find something very important in this short passage if we take a moment to notice that it speaks of *the grace of God [that] has appeared,* of *the blessed hope and the manifestation of ... Jesus Christ.* The former is something that has happened, the latter something that is yet to happen. Why is this particularly significant for us as Christians?

The moment we read this, we discern an essential difference between the context in which an early Christian saw him or herself and the context in which we see ourselves within our culture. For an early Christian, life was lived between two events, one remembered with joy and the other expected with ... (perhaps no single word expresses this adequately). The fact that Christ would appear again as Lord of all was taken with tremendous seriousness. It signified many things. It meant on a personal level that life was essentially accountable to his authority. It meant also that all creation was regarded as having a destiny, a purpose within the purposes of God; and this purpose was in the process of being fulfilled through Jesus Christ.

Thus we can see that Christian faith gave to human life a clear meaning. Life was lived between a glorious memory and a glorious hope. Christ had come in flesh, Christ would come as Lord and Judge. Contrast this to the rather pathetic wilderness of much contemporary living. Life is lived on a kind of island of fleeting time where even the relevance of secular history is questioned. We are encouraged to feel that what happened in the past doesn't really matter, and as for the future, nobody has the slightest idea — so why even think about it!

It is easy for us to assume that such wrestling with the meaning of life would not even be an issue in an ancient and apparently simpler world. Nothing could be further from the truth! We have only to notice how the writer speaks of the effort necessary *in the present age to live lives that are self-controlled, upright, and godly.* Could anything sound more contemporary? Any late twentieth-century Christian could find endless common ground with a man or woman who first read this letter or heard it read in some Christian gathering in the first century.

How did they see the consequences of what Jesus had done for them? Listen to their voices. *He it is who gave himself for us that he might redeem us from all iniquity and purify for himself a people of his own who are zealous for good deeds!* We look at the words *a people of his own,* and we realize how badly we need to redefine what it means to be a particular people who belong to Christ. What would this mean? We are told one thing it would mean — being *zealous for good deeds.* This can certainly refer to personal goodness of life, but it can also mean having the will and the capacity to act for good towards others and towards the society we live in.

A person living in such a way has a reason, a meaning, for living in the world caringly and generously. Where does this meaning come from? First, from believing that, by entering the world in Christ, God has called us into a body of faithful people who derive meaning and purpose in their lives from being members, limbs, of Christ's body. This conviction can be for each one of us *salvation* brought by *the grace of God* (v. 11). The second source of meaning comes from our belief that all of life, indeed all of creation, moves towards an accounting with God. For a Christian, the terms of this accounting will be in *the manifestation … of our Saviour, Jesus Christ.*

Two further insights from this short scripture.

Notice how the writer speaks of *the grace of God … training us … to live.* Here is a perception that has returned to Christian church life only in recent years. We are realizing that Christian formation, training, is a life-long process and ideally applies to every aspect of our living in the world.

To speak of *self-controlled* lives is to focus on the heart of the contemporary struggle for meaning. We live in a society determined to control every possible aspect of our lives. What we choose to buy, how we spend our leisure time, the way we perceive political decisions and policies — all are manipulated by forces that wish to control our responses. (To say this is not by any means to indulge in the paranoia of presuming that we are the victims of pernicious plots.) Even the phrase self-control needs to be seen through a Christian lens. What self will control? The old sinful self? Or the self that has been offered to the higher self of Christ as Lord?

The Gospel

In that region there were shepherds living ... keeping watch. We need to meet these people because they are the representatives of all of us on this night. If we want to go to Bethlehem, we have to go with them. To our knowledge, nobody else went. Eventually more exalted visitors came, but hardly on this same night — no matter how many Sunday school pageants say so!

They were *living in the fields,* and a dangerous living it was. They were tough men in a harsh world where encounters with angels were few and far between, if ever. Encounters were far more likely to be with rustlers and thieves who slit throats in the night hours and made off with a flock. Something formidable and impressive would be needed to get a response from these men, let alone to terrify them — in the way Luke describes.

An angel of the Lord stood before them, and the glory of the Lord shone around them. We can now choose to go through all the contortions of Western Christians, asking what this was and how it could be and what Luke can possibly be saying to us. This way lies frustration. Even more, this way is a profound betrayal of scripture. Instead, we need to recall those moments in our own experience when an angel appeared to us and glory shone around us, when the direction of our lives was changed and we were moved to journey to a place we had not been before, a sacred place, a place that for us became Bethlehem.

I have seen angels appear and glory shining around as I have watched modern young couples move through the baptism of their child when they themselves have only recently expressed interest in disinterring their own long-buried Christian faith. I have seen angels and glory shining in the pain-filled eyes of those who have discovered that there really is a grace that can become our ally in a time of great fear and anxiety. Angels and glory shine when we encounter someone who moves towards and through death with an extraordinary grace and dignity and courage.

The essential *"good news of great joy"* that these moments bring to often busy, and more often disbelieving, people is that something is born in their lives and in their experience that they had no idea existed. To take this ongoing and inner meaning from the text does not lessen the truth of the original glory that shone around those long-ago men in those distant fields to whom the original good news was given. On that night Mary gave birth to our Christ, and doubtless, Joseph did what he could to be of help to the woman he loved. So also it comes about that, day after day and night after night until the end of time, Christ struggles to be born in our human lives and our human experiences. We look in our various mirrors and we find we are the shepherds. We will realize that scripture's inexhaustible richness speaks to us on many levels. To those long-ago shepherds it spoke of *"a child wrapped ... lying in a manger"* — in other words, a child who would look deceptively ordinary. The words of this scripture can warn us that Christ comes to us again and again in the utterly ordinary things of our experience, and that, therefore, we need to be alert to the possibilities of his coming.

"Glory to God," sang the angels, and *"peace among those whom [God] favours."* Already, in these few shepherds, a small portion of humanity was favoured on that night of nights by a glimpse of God's glory. It is quite certain that you and I will be given such moments. They will most likely come when we are *in the fields* — those places where we live our daily lives. If we are open to such God-given moments, then they will bring us *peace,* for we will know that, beyond the realm we are so fond of calling real life, there is a realm even more real!

First Sunday after Christmas

1 Samuel 2:18–20, 26
Psalm 148
Colossians 3:12–17
Luke 2:41–52

Weavings

The quest for God is often involved in our search for what we love and want to hold or protect, or for what we feel we deeply need. Often we find that this quest leads us to the place where prayer is said and praise is offered.

First Reading. The parents of Samuel visit their son as he serves in the temple worship with the priest Eli.

The Psalm. As a crowd praises God in the temple, it becomes obvious that there is no limit to the reasons for praising God, no boundaries to the holiness of creation.

Second Reading. The quest for Christian community must look realistically at human nature, so that there is a clear picture of where and how it needs grace to transform it.

The Gospel. The parents of Jesus search for him and finally find him in the Temple area, surrounded by his elders and completely at home. In their search we can discern our own searching for Jesus as Lord.

Reflections

First Reading

This passage serves as an echo — perhaps we should say a fore-shadowing — of the gospel passage. In each one there is a child, his parents (feeling very different things and in very different moods!), and a priestly figure or figures.

There is something tender about this passage, as if the writer is especially won over by the picture of the child, his obviously doting (or slightly guilty) mother, and the old priest's annual blessing. Every year the boy's robe has been renewed: *His mother used to make for him a little robe and take it to him each year.* Here is a rather beautiful reminder to us that our relationship with God is to be, above all else, a growing one. Life is about growing towards God.

Samuel is *ministering before the Lord.* Here again is a reminder of something essential about Christian spirituality. What we are about each day is to develop the art — can we call it that? — of entering into the presence of God. It is easy to think of this art as the specialty of certain people (my priest in the parish church) while I, in my downtown office or suburban home, am far too involved in the world for such esoteric stuff! Yet spiritual growing is not just the vocation of someone thought of as a religious professional. Entering into the presence of God is possible for any Christian, if he or she is prepared to practise the art in simple ways and for short but consistent periods of time.

When Eli the priest speaks of *the gift that [Hannah] made to the Lord* (meaning her son Samuel), he is saying something that applies not only to Hannah and her husband Elkanah, but to all Christian parents. If we can speak of Christian parent-hood as a vocation, then this means nothing less than to bring our children *as a gift made to the Lord* — in other words, to do everything in one's power to give a child the gift of the presence and knowledge of God in his or her life.

The Psalm

If the camera lens had been invented when this psalm was written, we would have had a magnificent video. It would have had space shots borrowed from NASA —*praise the Lord from the heavens.* It would have ransacked the great paintings of the Renaissance for majestic winged creatures — *praise him all you angels of his.* We would then have been hurled through the solar system — *sun and moon* — and on through the galaxy — *all you shining stars.* We would even sail out on to the great aerial oceans that were once thought to be above the clouds as *waters above the heavens.*

Perhaps this is where a twentieth-century video would stop. After all, everything has been shown. But not so for us. Beyond the deepest heaven and the farthest stars, yet closer than our own souls, lies the ultimate beauty and majesty who *commanded and they were created,* the One who gave *a law which shall not pass away.*

We are caught again by the roving camera. This time we explore earth itself. We plunge into the oceans to encounter *sea-monsters and all deeps.* We are swept through weather systems and climates —*fire and hail, snow and fog, tempestuous wind.* All these are presented to us as something more than mere natural phenomena. They do not just exist. They are all *doing [God's] will.*

Now we climb *mountains and all hills.* We sweep through groves of *fruit trees and all cedars.* We run with *wild beasts and all cattle,* shrink from *creeping things,* and wonder at the grace of *wingèd birds.* Suddenly, we are in the human environment, its structures and institutions ruled by *princes and all rulers of the world.* Beyond them, never quite to be made prisoners of structures and authorities, are *young men and maid-*

ens, old and young together. Finally, our ears are deafened by the combined song of all creation, singing not of its own glory, but to the glory of God whose *splendour is over earth and heaven.*

With poetry like this psalm, no wonder the ancients believed that the stars sang! Perhaps they do, and it is our ears that need opening. Perhaps we need to be *a people who are near [to God.]*

Second Reading

When we read a long-ago Christian writer calling the people of a Christian community *God's chosen ones,* it pulls us up short. If it does not, it should. It shows us suddenly and vividly how easily we can take for granted that we are a member of a Christian congregation. Ask most people why they are in any particular congregation, and you may be told any of a dozen reasons. Ask them why they are Christian at all, and you will get a variety of answers. But you will almost never hear someone say, "Because God chose me."

We are not easy with such language. We may feel that we are assuming too much. Am I so significant in this vast order of things that God would have reason to single me out and choose me? Yet here is a New Testament writer telling us that this is precisely why we are in this congregation, baptized, or possibly thinking about baptism, as a Christian. What follows from seeing ourselves as in some sense chosen? We need to ask what we are chosen *for.* As soon as we ask this question, the realization hits that we must have been chosen to carry out a certain ministry. Then comes the responsibility to find out what specifically God wishes us to do.

The rest of this passage is, in effect, a description of the various gifts needed to form and hold a Christian community. And the implications of this description are witheringly realistic about us all! When the writer bids us, *Clothe yourselves with compassion, kindness, humility, and patience,* he does so for the very reason that these specific virtues are not necessarily always present in our dealings with each other! This is even more true of his plea to *forgive each other.* His repetition of the word *forgive* no less than three times in the same sentence is a measure of how necessary this appeal can be in congregational and in family life.

The admonition to *clothe yourselves with love* brings to mind an interesting thought about something else implied by the phrase. One has the image of a garment being intentionally put on. But surely this means that we must *choose* to love. This does not always come naturally. We have to be intentional about loving. The moment we see it this way, we realize how absolutely realistic this scripture is.

And be thankful. How simple it sounds. The writer does not elaborate with a single extra word. Perhaps because being thankful is so central to the whole enterprise of being Christian. Even more, it is central to the whole enterprise of being a human being!

Let the word of Christ dwell in you. Contrast this with what is so often true for many of us. We think of the word of Christ in a certain book. This is quite true. We can think of the word of Christ coming in a helpful sermon. Again true. But the word of Christ actually in me? Once again we are jolted into thinking about these things in a new way, seeing more clearly what it means to be Christian.

When we hear someone suggesting that we *teach and admonish one another,* we realize how we are reaching back to these very early Christians to help us in the task of being Christian today. It is again becoming true that we teach one another. Many congregations are rediscovering that the teaching ministry is not merely an ordained ministry. Wonderful things can be achieved when a community realizes that many of its members have this gift and, therefore, this ministry.

Lastly, there is a marvellous expansiveness to the last instruction. One can see the hands of the writer reaching widely before or after writing, *Whatever you do, in word or deed, do everything in the name of the Lord Jesus.* Being Christian may indeed be about doing various things — worshipping, praying, learning, and so on — but at the end of the day, it is not so much about doing as about being — being Christian with all of one's being. Then the doing follows.

The Gospel

The moment Luke tells us that *every year his parents went to Jerusalem for the festival,* we recall the image of Hannah and Elkanah making the same pilgrimage every year. The significance lies in the words *every year.* This scripture may be reminding us of the value of repeated rituals in our lives. We often smile indulgently at people who say, "We've always done it this way." And we may want to smile at the phrase, *they went up as usual for the festival.* We think how uninteresting life can be when it is just *as usual.* But, on the other hand, it is important to have some patterns of which we can say, "Good! We are doing it as usual!" Patterned life has order, a measure of relaxed expectation. We can, to a degree, depend on it. Sometimes the thing that keeps a person faithful is the memory of some repeated ritual done together as a family in earlier years. Rituals can give shape and resilient texture to our lives.

The story begins when the festival has ended. Every parent identifies with what happens. Each assumes the boy is with the other. They discover otherwise, feeling all the terror of any parent. We go with them on the breathless return journey, the frantic combing of the city, the mixture of anger and relief at finding him.

Another level of the story may be possible, a different telling of it. We too can make assumptions, not about the child Jesus but about Jesus as our Lord. We can assume that he is with us, that we can take his presence for granted somewhere in the coming and going of our full life. We have our lives to live, friends to cultivate, jobs to do. He will be there when we look for him. But something happens to make us realize that we need him — we need a resource, a grace beyond ourselves. Suddenly he is not there. Somewhere on the journey of being busy and achieving, we have lost touch with him. We begin to search. *They returned to Jerusalem to search for him.* The city where we search is large, uncaring, impersonal. But we must return to our own "Jerusalem," the centre of our lives. There we will find him.

This telling is one pattern we can take from the story. There are others. We could tell about experiencing a great loss of some kind, the kind of loss that banishes everything else from our thoughts. Nothing else matters but to deal with this loss. We seek in the huge city that is life today. We go in many directions — a recommended counsellor, a recommended book, a suggested holiday. Hither and yon we search. There may come a time when, having tried everything, we come seeking to the Temple, to the church itself, the institution that so often frustrates and angers us by failing to fulfil our expectations for it, by failing to conform to what we think it should be. Sometimes, to our great surprise, it is there that we find our Christ, the Christ we have been *searching for in great anxiety.* There are those for whom this has happened, who meet the Christ they are searching for in a half-forgotten collect said quietly at Evensong, in the steady flame of a candle on a distant altar, in the simplicity of a piece of bread placed in their hand, in the third verse of a remembered hymn.

Second Sunday after Christmas

Jeremiah 31:7–14
Psalm 147:13–21
Ephesians 1:3–14
John 1:(1–9) 10–18

Weavings

Throughout these readings, we hear God calling together those who formerly have been scattered and forming them into a people for God's own purposes.

First Reading. Lyrically and tenderly Jeremiah assures his fearful contemporaries that, even though they go into exile, return will become possible.

The Psalm. God's people have been gathered, and have been given a sense of identity and security, for which they give fervent praise.

Second Reading. Writing to the Christian community, Paul points to the continuing formation of a new people of God, to whom gifts are being given to be used for God's glory.

The Gospel. John tells us of the One who came, offered himself to his own people, was rejected, then, at great and glorious cost, gathered to himself a people for God.

Reflections

First Reading

Because the theme of the gathering of God's people runs all through these readings, we need to consider what this theme may mean for us as Christians today. These words of Jeremiah are spoken at a time when there was little evidence that anything remotely resembling what he hoped for would come true! Thousands of his people were already in captivity in Babylon, taken there by the Babylonian attack in 597 BC. He himself was in a very precarious position in Jerusalem. His warnings against foolish political decisions by the rulers of his nation had made it possible for them to label Jeremiah an enemy of his own people. Yet Jeremiah never gives way to a bitterness and cynicism that could so easily have been justified. He certainly allows himself to show anger, weariness, frustration. To do so was totally understandable.

To realize this about a person who faced immense social turmoil is in itself a lesson and example for us, as we read his book. In many ways, we today face what Jeremiah faced — great changes, many choices calling for our response, strident voices pointing to various solutions, deep divisions of thought and attitude, concern about the future. We too can at times feel angry, confused, and frustrated. As with Jeremiah, such reactions are perfectly understandable. From across the centuries, Jeremiah gives us an example of someone who never lost what we might call his sweetness of soul. The God whom we hear speaking through Jeremiah speaks with tenderness. *With consolations I will lead them back ... for I have become a Father to Israel.*

Jeremiah never lost hope. This may seem obvious, but it is another very important lesson for those of us who read him today. That he never lost hope is all the more remarkable because he was a very sensitive and emotional person. Jeremiah is many times devastated by the rejection and contempt that he receives, yet in spite of everything, he can summon up the inner strength to speak of a future joy as if it were already being experienced! *For the Lord has ransomed Jacob, and has redeemed him from hands too strong for him.*

It is important to recognize the reason for this inner strength. Jeremiah's fortitude arose from his understanding of the nature of God. God would be utterly faithful. There was not a shred of doubt in his mind about this. And more remarkable, even the disasters of the people are understood to be within the rule of God. *"He who scattered Israel will gather him."* Here is the solid foundation of Judaism. God is all in all. Not merely the God of the nice and easy parts of life. This does not mean that God, in some vicious whim, hurls his people into exile. Jeremiah would have understood that God's people, in the moral freedom and responsibility which is God's gift, had by their choices and actions made exile inevitable. Yet even here, God does not leave them destitute. *See, I am going to bring them from the land of the north ... They shall come and sing aloud on the height of Zion.*

This rock-like faith of Jeremiah teaches us that our own understanding of God is supremely important. According to who and what we understand God to be, we will engage life on that basis. To assume that we can give our trust to God is to become a person who can live on the basis of trust and who can come to relationships with an initial trustfulness. Our vision of God shapes our character and attitudes.

Nowhere is Jeremiah's sweetness of soul more obvious than in the way he speaks of his people returning. In his mind's eye, he sees them coming home. But he sees more than a huge amorphous straggle of refugees. He sees *among them the blind and the lame, those with child and those in labour together.* Take particular notice of that last lovely image formed by the word *together*. This is a people who have changed. They have discovered compassion in their exile experience. Even in the struggle of their return, they will have time to tend those among them who are needy and vulnerable. This is a people who have *found grace in the wilderness* (31:2).

In our wilderness of contemporary Christian experience, we would do well to consider the reason for our "exile." Is it that we, too, may be a people who are being called to discover grace and compassion in these difficult times?

The Psalm

Worship the Lord, O Jerusalem. We are celebrating the generosity of God. This is the whole point of worship. Worship being demanded of *Jerusalem* suggests something that we very often forget, or at least neglect. Worship is not merely personal. Because of the individualism of our age, we tend to fall into the trap of thinking that worship has a personal agenda. But here, a whole society is being called to worship. This is a lesson we are being harshly taught by Islam today. We watch as whole societies bow before the God who, above all else, demands submission. The very word *Islam* means submission.

Notice again in this psalm how God acts in all that takes place, not just in some events that are suitably selected to reflect credit on God! On the one hand, this God *has blessed your children ... has established peace on your borders ... satisfies you with the finest wheat.* On the other hand, this same God causes us to say fearfully, *Who can stand against his cold?* Here is God in majesty and power. And now that God is seen to wield ultimate authority over creation, we must also yield to God's ultimate moral authority. *He declares his word to Jacob, his statutes and his judgements to Israel.* This God is entirely in control.

Second Reading

In a sentence, Paul is addressing the community in Ephesus and asking them if they really know who they are and what they have been given. As we read this passage, we are being asked the same questions. Do we really know who we are and what we have been given? There are many signs among today's Christians that we have largely forgotten. Or, if we remember, we take these things for granted.

Paul points out no less than seven spiritual blessings that we possess as Christians. First of all, God *chose us in Christ ... to be holy and blameless.* To contemplate these words, even for a moment, is to realize with a shock how far we are from this quality of spiritual life. Next, God *destined us for adoption as his children through Jesus Christ.* This passage tells us who we really are. In the words of the old catechism, I am nothing less than "a member of Christ, the child of God, and an inheritor of the kingdom of heaven." How deeply precious this self-definition must be for we who live in a society that spends millions of dollars trying to persuade us of our essential identity as consumers!

Paul continues his list. In Christ *we have redemption through his blood, the forgiveness of our trespasses.* This verse contains a particularly lovely English word — Christ has *lavished [this] on us.* Again, a moment's contemplation shows us the nature of what we have been given. My being Christian means that I am accepted by this most holy God, in spite of my abysmal spiritual and moral poverty. This acceptance is given freely as a gift of God, and if we are prepared to accept a very simple image, it is handed to me in the pierced hands of Jesus who stands between me and the throne of this holy God.

[God] has made known to us the mystery of his will ... to gather up all things in [Christ.] What words can one find to express this greatest of mysteries about Christian faith? Some-

how, almost beyond language, Jesus is my window on to the universe. His life, death, and resurrection are offered to me as a kind of lens through which I view all reality, all time, all creation, seeing in him and through him that love dwells at the heart of things, and that this love can never be overcome.

Again Paul returns to his thought of our being destined by God, this time to receive the gift of Jesus as a kind of *inheritance*. And now we are given the reason for our being given these gifts. We are being asked for a response. The gifts are given *so that we ... might live for the praise of [Christ's] glory.* At this stage, we are suddenly made to realize that we have been presented with nothing less than a list of our baptismal blessings. *When you had heard the word of truth, the gospel of your salvation, and had believed in [Christ], [you] were marked with the seal of the promised Holy Spirit.*

The Gospel

The power of familiarity to diminish a great insight is seen perhaps nowhere so clearly as in the opening sentence of this passage. He was in the world, and the world came into being through him; yet the world did not know him. At unimaginable cost, God becomes human only to have the sublime gesture brutally rejected, and to encounter death in one of its most terrible forms. John is not able to leave his utterance of tragedy with just single sentence. He repeats it in another form. *He came to what was his own, and his own people did not accept him.*

But. The single small word sounds like a trumpet in this setting. It makes all the difference. It is a shaft of light in darkness. It shouts that all is not lost. Some did receive the gesture. Some recognized the divine in the human countenance. Some responded. With these, God in Christ has entered into relationship. *But to all who received him ... he gave power to become children of God.*

Suddenly we are confronted with a people. They have been called into being by the costly gesture of God in Christ. John paints a vast canvas in these next few verses. At the centre is our Lord. The eye cannot help but be drawn to him. One is reminded of the great mosaics of the Orthodox world, where the Christ Pantocrator — ruler of creation — occupies the centre point, and everything else takes its existence from him and moves in his orbit. *We have seen his glory ... From his fullness we have all received, grace upon grace.*

But John goes even further in this sublime statement. Through the majesty of the scene that John is painting, Christ radiates power and energy. Everything else has life only because of Christ. I suddenly become aware that this is true of my own existence. In a mysterious sense, this is the power and energy on which I draw for my existence. This is the great sun around which my life revolves and from whom I take this life, receiving *grace upon grace.*

But there is even more. It is easily missed, because it comes in the very last line of the passage. As I stand with John and look at the vast panorama of creation with Christ at its centre, John quietly tells me that I am not yet seeing the ultimate heart of reality, the ultimate source of power. John says, *No one has ever seen God. It is God the only Son, who is close to the Father's heart, who has made him known.* I listen, not so much understanding as worshipping, and I hear of unimaginable glory. And in the words, *close to the Father's heart,* I am also learning where I will ultimately find the mystery that we call Love.

Epiphany of the Lord

Isaiah 60:1–6
Psalm 72:1–7, 10–14
Ephesians 3:1–12
Matthew 2:1–12

Weavings

In all these scriptures appointed for this feast day, a great gift is being given.

First Reading. The people of God have been given the great gift of their freedom. Now they must learn how to use it in God's service.

The Psalm. The psalmist prays for the gift of justice for the newly crowned king. The hope is that, having received the gift, he will use it and so reflect the face of a God of justice.

Second Reading. Paul speaks of a gift so tremendous that it is almost unbelievable. The riches of Christ know no limits, and they are offered to all as a gift.

The Gospel. Coming from the East, surviving the dangers of Herod's court, the magi arrive at the place where the Child lies, and they offer their gifts.

Reflections

First Reading

On both sides of the Atlantic, a poet is often asked to compose a special work to mark a great point of change in a nation's history, whether it be an inauguration or a coronation. I think we can understand this passage best when we treat it as a similar kind of poem.

It looks as if the long exile in Babylon is over. But so recent is their freedom that the people cannot quite believe it, and Isaiah wants them to realize that the future shines ahead and calls them to plan and to work. His first line is almost literally a jolt, an electrifying shout: *Arise, shine; for your light has come, and the glory of the Lord has risen upon you.* There is much more involved in Isaiah's vision than the fate of a single small people. This new found freedom, this opportunity to build the future, is nothing less than the gift of God, and the significance of the gift must not be missed. The matter in hand is not Israel's glory but God's glory.

Consider for a moment a very contemporary nuance in this passage. Isaiah points out to his generation that their young people are coming home from Babylon: *Your sons shall come from far away, and your daughters shall be carried on their nurses' arms.* (I think if I were a woman listening to this passage, I would be tempted to ask Isaiah if he really meant that daughters were any less capable of walking home than sons!) All levity aside — the image of young people returning to build the future reminds us of an appalling situation in our own time. Even when every sign of the economy is indicating prosperity and growth — *the abundance of the sea ... brought to you ... the wealth of nations shall come to you* — we still show no signs of being able to build a world where millions of young people will be employed!

If this passage were to be used for a homily at Epiphany, I would suggest that we see a parallel between the people of God long ago being given back not only their land and their city but also their sense of identity, and the Christian people of God being given the gift of our Lord. Just as Isaiah's listeners needed to understand what their gift meant — new hope and new possibilities — so we have to realize what the timeless gift of our Lord means in hope and spiritual possibilities for us.

The Psalm

Whenever a new head of state takes office, we regard it as quite normal to hear him or her make certain promises. They will be phrased differently, depending on the person assuming high office or the conditions of the country at the time. But the promises will always have certain constant themes. The new ruler will promise to be a person of integrity, to be concerned for all the people rather than some element within the society. In a word, his or her promise will be to be a good head of state.

There may be another element in these promises. Often new rulers will acknowledge that they stand before a higher court than human society. They take their authority from God. When we ask where these customs come from, we turn to the Bible. This psalm is one of the most explicit statements about the source of authority in society. *Give the king your justice, O God.* But why this prayerful request? For one purpose — that the king may *rule your people righteously and ... with justice.*

The people are not the possession of the ruler. The people, says the psalmist, are *your [God's] people.* Millennia before we ever hear language such as "having a preferential option for the poor," this psalm emphasizes the cause of *the needy ... the poor.* Only if this cause is pursued will the society be one where *the righteous flourish;* and *there shall be an abundance of peace.* The moral integrity of such a society will make it a blessing among other nations.

Christians look for righteousness and peace within the ministry of our Lord. We see the vision in his words again and again. No earthly society can ever rise completely to his moral challenge, but our never-ending hope that these values will not disappear from public life is based solidly on the light that streams at this season from the Christ who has accepted the poverty of coming among us.

Second Reading

It is easy to miss the immensity of the concept Paul is trying to convey to his readers in this passage. He wisely takes a few lines building up to it. By using the word *mystery* no less than three times, he draws our attention and curiosity. It is impossible not to ask, "What is this mystery?" Like a good story teller, he suggests that it has been hidden from others but is now about to be revealed to his listeners: *In former generations this mystery was not made known ... it has now been revealed.*

When the mystery was revealed, it was indeed astounding for those who heard it. For Jewish followers of Jesus, it could also have been deeply troubling. The mystery was that the new faith in Jesus as Christ knew no limits whatsoever! It was for the world — nothing less. As it is true that *God [has] created all things,* so it is now true that faith in the person known as God's son is offered and is accessible to all men and women. I am inclined to think that this passage addresses us especially these days in an increasingly multicultural world. Perhaps it is more true to say, an increasingly multicultural *society.* After all, the world has always been multicultural! We just did not realize this fully; and if we did, it was through visiting other cultures but returning home to the known and familiar.

More and more we talk about possible future relationships between the great religions now mingling in our streets. Yet before we talk about this, we need perhaps to remind ourselves that, within the many races sharing our local shopping centre, there are also many Christians! We can sympathize with the difficulty that the Jewish people of Paul's time may have had in realizing that Christ knows no boundaries of race. Paul speaks of *the wisdom of God in its rich variety*. The evidence for this is all around us.

Of this gospel I have become a servant, says Paul. The question we need to ask is whether we ourselves have become a servant of this gospel, whether we are prepared to accept this great mystery of the Christ of no boundaries.

The Gospel

After Jesus was born ... wise men from the East came to Jerusalem. Who they were, what they did in their society, where precisely they came from, why they made this journey — none of these questions has ever been answered. Guesses and probabilities abound, but no more. Because we know so little about them, these travellers have become figures of high and endless romance. One of the most haunting expressions of their journey is "The Coming of the Magi" by T.S. Eliot, and it might possibly be useful for this Sunday, perhaps read by more than one voice.

Everything about their journey provides rich material for reflecting on our own Christian journey. We begin at the first parallel between their lives and ours — they journeyed, as do we. Does this make us wise? It would seem so, if travelling means that we experience constant change in our lives, and that we are continually deepening and maturing. Refusal to do this kind of inner travelling can result in a shallow and limited spiritual life.

We observed his star at its rising. This season of the church year is trying to get us to do precisely this — to become aware of Christ as a kind of star, a shining light that calls us to travel towards it.

In the time of King Herod. The old king signifies everything that is the enemy of this journey. He wishes that the journey had never taken place, and he is determined to end it or to use it for his own purposes. In our own spiritual journey there are danger points. Herod turns up in many disguises. Many things conspire to halt or side-track our journey towards our Lord. Most of them are deceptively ordinary things — business, weariness, depression, anxiety, cynicism.

When they had heard the king, they set out. For some reason I like the sound of *they set out.* There is a hint that they knew they had been side-tracked. We too need to realize when we have been distracted from our journey, when we have left the main highway for attractive detours that end in *cul de sacs!* Then we need to recoup, turn around, and once again *set out,* realizing that, although we may have chosen another direction, our "star" did not, and that we need to look for it again.

On entering the house ... they knelt down and ... offered him gifts. This scene is engraved on the minds of most people from innumerable children's pageants! But the same scene speaks to the depths of our human experience. It is absolutely necessary in life to have something for which we are prepared to search, to risk, and when we find it, to bow down and offer our gifts. If that something is worthy and good and pure, then we are indeed rich. We are, one might say, kings.

For a Christian, the ultimate reality to journey towards and to search for, is our Lord Jesus Christ. If and when we find this presence in our lives, our instinct is to bow down and offer the best that is in us, the gifts we bring. It is easy to forget that the gifts we have were given by God in the first place. When we lay them before Jesus as our Lord, we are merely returning what we have been given. But even so, we grow in the giving. For in the enterprise of giving, we somehow touch the mystery of that greatest of journeys — the journey of God.

Baptism of the Lord: Proper 1

Isaiah 43:1–7
Psalm 29
Acts 8:14–17
Luke 3:15–17, 21–22

Weavings

Throughout these readings, the voice of God is heard naming those who are being called to God's service. This calling is accompanied by the gift of God's Holy Spirit.

First Reading. God calls a people by name and assures them that they are indeed the people of God.

The Psalm. On every side, throughout all nature, the voice of God is heard. This theme is echoed by the voices of a people united in God's praise.

Second Reading. The apostles journey to where some people have already made a Christian commitment, and they find this commitment confirmed by the coming of the Holy Spirit.

The Gospel. John the Baptist expects the coming of the Holy Spirit, and finds his expectation borne out in the events of Jesus' baptism.

Reflections

First Reading

So often in the writings of the prophets, we see a wonderful use of the simple word *but.* Almost always it heralds a great change of mood, a great change in the news about to be proclaimed. *But now* can be a hinge moment between condemnation and affirmation — between the admonition that Israel must pay a price for falling away from God, and the assurance that in spite of everything God will act on behalf of his people. This is one of those moments.

Do not fear. One cannot help wondering if the words spoken by the angel to Mary are an echo in the New Testament of these beautiful and simple words that had brought comfort to God's people so often in their history, and have since brought comfort to countless men and women to whom they have been spoken.

I have redeemed you; I have called you by name, you are mine. There is a rhythm in what is said here, a quiet lyrical succession of phrases that together become deeply assuring. They could be a pattern for anyone trying to reach out to another in need of assurance and strengthening.

When you pass through the waters, I will be with you. How beautifully these words link with the moment in which Jesus stands in the Jordan and discovers that the Spirit validates his journey south to that place. If we are prepared to link the next images to our Lord's experience, we find ourselves thinking of his future suffering — the fire of agony through which he must walk, the flames of fear and hatred that threaten to consume him. *When you walk through fire you shall not be burned, and the flame shall not consume you.*

As we consider the things that God is prepared to give for his people, to sacrifice for their rescue, we cannot help but realize what has been given and sacrificed by our Lord to make possible our own salvation. *I give Egypt as your ransom, Ethiopia and Seba ... I give people in return for you.* To hear these words as a Christian is to be reminded that our Lord has given life itself to call us to himself.

Now we see a people being gathered, near and distant, young and old. We should not neglect the mention of the four directions *from the east ... from the west ... I will say to the north ... and to the south ... "bring my sons from far away and my daughters from the ends of the earth."* Such images are most important for us who wonder about the seeming decline of Christian faith in the Western world. We are being reminded here that our view of Christian faith must be planet-wide. Then we begin to see the hosts of people being called to Christian faith in our time, *everyone who is called by my name, whom I created for my glory.*

The Psalm

We are singing a song that points to God as the ruler of creation and rejoices in the fact. *The Lord is upon the mighty waters ... breaks the cedars of Lebanon ... makes Lebanon skip ... splits the flames of fire ... shakes the wilderness ... strips the forests bare.* We sing these verses today with a sense of being chastened by our long ignoring of God's lordship over creation. We are being made to bow before a greater power than our own, as we begin to realize the grave consequences of our behaviour towards the natural environment.

The psalmist's image, *In the temple of the Lord all are crying, "Glory!",* is not possible in our fragmented society. Still it is becoming increasingly obvious that, unless we regard the created order as the possession of a power higher than our own, as a sacred trust for our care and not merely our glory and enrichment, we shall be in great trouble. Our prayer might be that the planet itself become the temple in which humanity as a whole stands and gives glory to a God who transcends humanity and the creation.

Because this vision cannot be made real in the foreseeable future, it is necessary continually that there be those who accept responsibility for offering creation back to God, for offering humanity and all its gifts and powers to God. One way to do this is by worship, by ascribing glory to God alone, by rejoicing in the role of being stewards of God in creation. Those who are prepared to offer themselves for this work are a people to whom God will *give strength* and *the blessing of peace.*

Second Reading

Perhaps it would be a help to describe the situation in which people like Peter and John found themselves. We have only to look back a little in this chapter to realize how they must have felt. They must still have been shaken by the brutal death of Stephen. Suddenly the high stakes of their involvement in this movement had become clear. Following that death, many of the Jerusalem community had scattered in various directions, trying to find communities where they could better blend in and have a reasonable measure of safety. All of this was threatening and discouraging.

At the same time, the most extraordinary things were happening to give encouragement and hope for the future. On every hand, people were being drawn to the new movement. Philip's work in Samaria was having amazing results. When we read that *Samaria had accepted the word of God, they sent Peter and John to them,* we can assume at least two possibilities. The first is that the use of the term *Samaria* (as distinct from something like *many in Samaria)* tends to suggest a widespread positive response to Philip's work. The second possibility is that neither Peter nor John, nor the rest of the Jerusalem community, can do anything but respond positively in turn to the obvious enthusiasm of the people. It would seem that a lot of things are not in their hands or under their control!

Does any of this sound familiar? The situation in today's church is very like what we see in this scripture. On the one hand, there is a chastened feeling in the life of the church. We are not suffering terrible things like martyrdom, but we are experiencing a great sense of frustration, and even fear, as we struggle to respond to the new realities of society and the needs of people. On the other hand, there are exciting and promising developments occurring in many congregations, aspects of renewal that have not come from the central planning of the denomination, but seemingly from a new spirit within the congregation itself. Many voices speak of these instances of renewal as the work of the Holy Spirit.

Turning back to the scripture, we note how Peter and John, representing the community as a whole, expect that baptism would normally be followed by some signs of the influence of the Holy Spirit. They do not seem to have been afraid of this, or to have wished to limit it in any way. There is a phrase in this scripture that should make us thoughtful: *They had only been baptized in the name of the Lord Jesus.* The word *only* should give us pause. What does this tell us about the relationship between baptism and the work of the Holy Spirit? While there is a prayer within our baptismal service that the Holy Spirit may indeed work in the life of the newly baptized, this scripture may be asking us to make much more of this continuing relationship, especially as we prepare adults for baptism.

The Gospel

The two words *expectation* and *questioning* leap out of this page of scripture to our time and experience. The people were focused on the figure and voice of John the Baptist. They expected something to emerge in that moment of history that would radically change their lives and their country. The question was whether John was this expected agent of great change, this Messiah.

John responded to the question without the least hesitation. He was not this expected agent of change. But he speaks immediately of One who is about to show himself. He is not only of far greater quality than John himself — *I am not worthy to untie the thong of his sandals* — but his coming will have consequences that those listening may not relish! There is a chilling sound to what John tells the crowd. *He will baptize you with the Holy Spirit and fire. His winnowing fork is in his hand.* This coming will entail a disturbing element of judgement. It will require life-changing choices. It will demand sacrifices.

Even as John is still speaking, Jesus comes south from the anonymity of Nazareth, enters the river, and offers himself to be baptized. In that moment, Jesus makes himself the model for what he asks of us who would follow him. Jesus *was praying*. He reaches out to God as a source of grace and strength and guidance beyond himself, and so he demands of us that we reach out to him in self-commitment, as we seek strength beyond our own strength to live in the world.

We have expectations and questions about every aspect of our lives — personal, professional, political. We are well aware that we are passing through massive transitions in every aspect of life. We know, too, that these transitions will bring — are already bringing — much turmoil to lives and relationships, to organizations and systems of every kind. High prices are already being paid for the great changes we are experiencing.

We are becoming increasingly aware — both within and far beyond the Christian community — that, if we are to move through the immediate future, we will need a source of strength beyond our own. Just as John points beyond himself to another who is greater, so each one of us needs to point to *one who is more powerful than I.* We seek the coming of that greater One into our lives. For a Christian, this must be our Lord Jesus Christ. With that coming, we receive a deep sense of peace about what our lives are given to us for — *the Holy Spirit descended upon him ... like a dove.* And we are also given the grace to know who we are —*"You are ... the Beloved; with you I am well pleased."*

Across the centuries, we also hear again the empowering words of Isaiah as they speak to us: *I have called you by name, you are mine.*

Second Sunday after the Epiphany: Proper 2

Isaiah 62:1–5
Psalm 36:5–10
1 Corinthians 12:1–11
John 2:1–11

Weavings

Woven through these readings is the theme of the generosity of God shown in gifts that God gives.

First Reading. In the image of a marriage between God and his people, Isaiah shows God delighting in his people and offering gifts of vindication and salvation.

The Psalm. A loving God offers refuge, food, and drink. For God's people, God is the well of life.

Second Reading. There are varieties of gifts, but they are all given by the Holy Spirit.

The Gospel. There is a guest at the wedding who can respond to a great need. Apart from the gift of his presence, Jesus gives the gift of wine.

Reflections

First Reading

In an interview, Alan Jones, who at the time of writing was dean of the Cathedral in San Francisco, was asked about the spiritual resources of his life. He replied that the Latin text of John 3:16 had always spoken deeply. It begins with the words, *"Sic Deus delexit"* (God so delights in the world). The moment he heard this, Jones realized that, if God delights in the world, then God delighted in him as a child of God. Ever since, this thought has seen him through some tough times.

The prophet hears God speaking as a lover and a newly married husband. In this case, the bride is the Jewish people. *As the bridegroom rejoices over the bride, so shall your God rejoice over you.* We Christians often speak of Christ as the bridegroom, the Church being his bride. There are certain lovely consequences that may flow from this. When two people deeply in love look at one another, they see each other differently from the way others see them. Each for the other is transformed. If our Lord and the church really do exist in this kind of relationship, then our Lord's view of the church will be extremely different from our human view. This thought may be very important these days when our human view of the church can be extremely jaundiced!

Our conversation about the church these days is full of frustration, fear for the future, and even anger that the church seems unable to fulfil all our hopes and intentions for it. We endlessly list its weaknesses as we see them, and we make dire prophecies about the future. But suppose that our Lord sees the church through very different eyes, looking at it from a heart that loves the church beyond measure — because he gave his life to bring it to birth. Could our Lord possibly see some reasons to delight in the church today? If this were true, then we badly need to discover our Lord's viewpoint. We need to make his eyes our eyes.

You shall be called by a new name that the mouth of the Lord will give. How do we begin to give the church a new name? What might this mean? Maybe rephrasing the verse slightly will allow it to speak to us. To talk about anything is to name it. When we talk scathingly about anything, we have named it worthy of contempt. On the other hand, when we choose to talk about something enthusiastically, we have named it worthy of appreciation. Perhaps our question needs to ask, What *new name* does our Lord wish us to give his church? Perhaps he wishes us to look at it, and to speak about it, as if we loved it passionately!

You shall be a crown of beauty in the hand of the Lord ... a royal diadem. Perhaps we need to look at the church with the express intention of discerning those things that are its crown jewels. We might begin in a very simple and personal way. What for oneself are the precious and lovely things of the church? A glorious anthem remembered clearly. A magnificent prayer that has entered into one's own speech patterns. A friendship discovered in the fellowship of the church. A deep sense of peace as a piece of bread is placed in one's hand. A cross, perhaps old and dulled by time, yet glorious against an evening sky. These and other things are the jewels that form *a crown of beauty ... a royal diadem.*

Through the words of Isaiah, God gives assurance to Israel that *you shall be called My delight Is in Her.* God has given the nation a new name. To say that God's delight is in her transforms the value of the nation. This does not suggest that the nation is perfect. It means that whatever the nation may be — unworthy, fearful, indecisive, even profoundly cynical and unbelieving and self-serving — God nevertheless delights in her, because God's vision is of the nation transformed! God sees the nation not as it is, but as it can be. Is this what we are called to do as we wrestle with our difficult relationship to today's church?

Your land [shall be called] Married. Notice in this verse (4) the contrast between naming Israel "Forsaken" or naming it "Married." There is nothing in between. There is no possibility of just having what we would call "an affair." Many people today think that they can have an affair with the church, using it when they need it, attending on special or uplifting occasions, following an admired leader, but otherwise withdrawing. In this scripture, there is no room for half-heartedness. It is a distinct choice — forsake or marry. Scripture can be chillingly stern and, at the same time, refreshingly clear!

The Psalm

It is easy to forget, or to be completely unaware of, the spiritual quality of what one is reading in this psalm. Here is a people prepared to speak of God in terms of *love* and *faithfulness, righteousness* and *justice* — even though their experiences in history could easily crush all such illusions. How do they preserve the ability to sing this song? They sing it because they are utterly convinced that such words speak truly of the nature of God. They are saying, or singing, that however things seem in life — and sometimes they seem very far from *love* and *faithfulness, righteousness* and *justice* — these things are indestructible because they are grounded in God. This is what they mean when they sing of God's love as something that *reaches to the heavens*, of God's justice being *like the great deep,* and of God's love being *priceless.*

Now we are given (v. 8,9) the images of this God's generosity, which link the psalm with the other three readings. God is *the well of life* from whom comes the gifts we need to serve

God, the gifts that are listed in the epistle passage. The images of God giving us *drink from the river of [God's] delights* take us to the conviviality and the expansive joy of the wedding in Cana.

Second Reading

Now concerning spiritual gifts, brothers and sisters. There are a couple of reasons why it would be a pity to rush into this passage and leave these opening words behind. We need to remember the kind of people to whom Paul was writing. The Corinthian community was, for the most part, affluent, sophisticated, and cosmopolitan. Many of its people would be exceedingly sure of themselves socially and intellectually. Think of the jolt some of them would receive upon hearing that their abilities and gifts are *spiritual gifts,* given from outside themselves and not in the least due to their own brilliance!

The second reason to look at these opening words is that Paul calls the Corinthians *brothers and sisters.* Significantly, all was by no means sweetness and light in this church. In fact, it was what we today would call dysfunctional. Divisions abounded. Exploitation was widespread, as was snobbery. Yet in spite of this, Paul preserved the bonds of community in Christ. This is a reminder for us today, as we seek to live in Christian community with so many conflicting opinions and visions and attitudes. Recently the English theologian Elizabeth Templeton, reflecting about the clashing of different visions in today's church, remarked that her Christian task was to remember that somehow she had to get to heaven with Ian Paisley! She added that, to get the point, each of us might think of the person we find most difficult to get along with.

Paul now hears people saying, *Let Jesus be cursed.* We are not sure what this refers to. Did he hear someone speaking like this in the gathering? Did he overhear it being said in the marketplace, by a member of the community who was trying to hide his or her allegiance? Was it a drunken throw-off remark?

We don't know, but this does not mean that the verse cannot speak to us. Succinctly, it tells us to be careful how we speak about our Lord. In a time when there are endless books about Jesus, endless theories about who he was — what he said or did not say, how he thought about his own identity — we need to be on the alert for anything we may say that appears to diminish his claim on us as Lord. While we can discuss endlessly *how* Jesus is risen, we commit ourselves to the fact that he *is* indeed risen. We can be open to many theories as to *how* he is Lord, as long as we have no doubt that he *is* Lord. To believe the latter is a gift of the Holy Spirit. *No one can say "Jesus is Lord" except by the Holy Spirit.*

Varieties of gifts but the same Spirit ... varieties of activities, but it is the same God who activates all of them in everyone. Every word of this statement is important for Paul. It is the very thing these people find so difficult to see. It is the very thing many Christians today find so difficult to accept. A congregation is not only a community of people, it is a community of widely differing gifts. This is the source of congregational richness, congregational health, congregational strength and vitality! It cannot be said too often. A congregation that is open to differences is potentially wealthy in the Spirit. Failure to recognize this, or tending to see differences as a threat, is to invite congregational poverty.

We need to remember, too, that the very richness of Paul's list, his reiteration of the words *to another ... to another ... to another,* emphasizes that every gift is no more and no less than other gifts. Above all, no single gift, no matter how intense or how captivating, has the right to dismiss other gifts or to think of them as lesser.

The Gospel

One is constantly startled at the way that scripture gives more each time one comes to it. In reading this passage aloud, I realized for the first time how often I was being confronted by the figure of our Lord's mother. First of all, I am told by John that *the mother of Jesus was there.* The fact that *Jesus and his disciples had also been invited* sounds almost as if their being there were an extension of an invitation that was primarily hers. When disaster strikes — because to run out of wine was a social disaster at a wedding — our Lord's mother is once again the main figure. *The mother of Jesus said to him, "They have no wine."*

Jesus' reply is extraordinarily passive, almost sullen — again suggesting that, whatever his relationship with these people, he feels no deep commitment on this occasion. *"What concern is that to you and to me? My hour is not yet come."* She merely turns and directs the servants, *"Do whatever he tells you."* There is something about this simple direction that makes us wonder if she knows something about him that he does not yet know himself. Is this moment a kind of test, subtly put to him by the woman who knows him better than any living soul, an invitation to discover who and what he is? In the end of the day, is it to Mary that we must give our thanks for the wine he brings? Every indication points to the fact that there would not have been any wine had she not applied her gentle pressure.

We know what happens next. The great jars are filled, wine flows, voices are lifted in joyous conversation, faces are flushed. We can hear the slightly inebriated voice of the steward as he compliments the bridegroom on the quality of the wine, the wink and the nudge as he speaks of those who serve *the good wine first, and then the inferior after the guests have become drunk.*

If what I have said about our Lord's mother speaks to us in any way, then this scripture seems to be offering a truth about a certain aspect of our lives. All of us can be grateful to others — perhaps not even remembered — who at various moments in our lives drew us further than we were prepared to go, and thereby helped us to discover gifts and powers that otherwise we would not have known. Mary knew her son. Perhaps she intuitively knew the wondrous reality that was in him, even as someone who loved us knew the lesser but nevertheless precious reality hidden in us.

Notice, too, that the pots of water were there *for the Jewish rites of purification* — for the washing of hands and, later, the washing of vessels. This water was for no exalted purpose. It is the supreme gift of our Lord to take the ordinary and to make from it something extraordinary. This is particularly true when the wine runs out in various ways in our lives. Joy, the wine of life, can go from us. It can go from a job, a relationship, a marriage — from anything in which we are involved. At such a time we may realize, as Mary does, that there is a guest in our lives who has the capacity to take what we have always dismissed as ordinary in ourselves, gifts whose value we have never realized, and to turn these things into rich resources.

Often when we have been through a desert time in life, but then discover unrealized gifts within us, we find ourselves turning in thanks to our Lord and saying, *"You have kept the good wine until now."*

Third Sunday after the Epiphany: Proper 3

Nehemiah 8:1–3, 5–6, 8–10
Psalm 19
1 Corinthians 12:12–31a
Luke 4:14–21

Weavings

Each of these scriptures speaks of gathering a people around a particular centre that has been formed and given by God.

First Reading. Just returned from exile, the people of Israel are called to gather to hear the code of the law read aloud by Ezra, one of their leaders.

The Psalms. Just as the law of God can be a central point for unifying a people, so also it can gather and give unity to the various elements in an individual.

Second Reading. Searching for a way to describe the complex nature of a community, Paul chooses the image of the human body itself as a principle of gathering.

The Gospel. At the outset of his ministry, Jesus reads aloud Isaiah's gathering call to serve of others, then offers himself as the embodiment of service.

Reflections

First Reading

All the people gathered together into the square before the Water Gate. Because we know that they had just returned from long exile, we can make a fair try at guessing their feelings as they gathered. They were engaged in a massive effort to put their country back together and rebuild their sacred city, after the trauma of being conquered and torn away from their home. One moment in Canadian history gives us a sense of this other long-ago moment. On the evening of 30 October 1995, a referendum was being held in Quebec to decide on the province's relationship with the rest of the country. An immense crowd from across the country gathered in the centre of Montreal. Unseen, but even more significant, a vast number of people were glued to their television sets, waiting to see if they would have a country when they woke up in the morning.

They told the scribe Ezra to bring the book of the law of Moses, which the Lord had given to Israel. While they had been in exile in Babylon, they had begun to pay great attention to their traditions written in the scrolls. Much work had been done. Through these scrolls the voice of God spoke to them, and the will of God for them was revealed. It was a natural thing to do, now that much work had been put in progress, to assemble as a people to hear that voice and to pledge themselves to do God's will. At times of crisis and rebuilding, a people can do well to let their past inform their future, by listening for the will of God speaking to them through the voice of their history and traditions.

The scene is vividly set for us. *The priest Ezra brought the law before the assembly ... He read from it ... from early morn-*

*ing until midday, in the presence of the men and the women ...
He was standing above all the people.* This is a carefully planned
event. Authority is being communicated. Ezra and the other
leaders stand well above the crowd. The law is presented as au-
thoritative, but human authority is also emphasized. A highly
centralized power group is present, and their names are listed
(v. 4). That this elaborate image of power and authority had an
effect is shown in the fact that *all the people stood up.*

After the law has been read, no time is lost in making sure
that the people understand it as the leadership elite wishes it to
be understood. We are told that *[the Levites] ... read from the
book, from the law of God, with interpretation ... They gave
the sense, so that the people understood.* We are witnessing a
highly political moment. Strong leadership is consolidating its
role.

Perhaps the most significant aspect of this long-ago event
for us is what it points to in our own culture and time. In many
ways our society, moving through great transition, is seeking
also for resources that transcend our own resources. We may
not use the explicit language of scripture. Millions may not even
be prepared to use the name of God! Nevertheless, the search
for grace and guidance is obvious on every side.

The Psalm

In this wonderful and ancient song, the glory of the sun and the
glory of God's law become mirrored in each other. Both em-
body the divine perfection. *The heavens declare the glory of
God ... The law of the Lord is perfect.* Both possess a certainty,
an utter dependability. *[The sun] goeth forth from the uttermost
edge of the heavens ... to the end of it again ... The judgements
of the Lord are true and righteous altogether.* Both are a source
of joy in life. *[The sun] rejoices like a champion to run its course
... The statutes of the Lord are just and rejoice the heart.* As the

sun is the source of light, so *the commandment of the Lord is clear and gives light to the eyes.* All of the vast created order, the environment and nourishment for our living, expresses the life and joy and glory of God.

In verses 7–11 we hear a voice singing of a source of grace in human experience that is beyond that experience itself. The law of God gives grace in various ways. It *revives the soul ... gives wisdom ... rejoices the heart ... gives light to the eyes.* To those who possess it, *there is great reward.* For a Christian reading this psalm, these properties of the Law may be seen as gifts that flow to us from our Lord. He is our Torah. He is the source that revives our souls, offers wisdom, provides light for our way. To know him and to follow him is to receive a great reward. Above all, it is through our Lord that *"the words of my mouth and the meditations of my heart be acceptable in [God's] sight."*

Second Reading

Of all the epistles we have from his hand, this letter to Corinth may well have been the most difficult for Paul to write. It was necessary to be stern. Things had gone very wrong. Paul is trying to give these people some vision of what a Christian community could and should be. Just as we begin reading this part of the letter, he introduces an image of Christian community that remains as vivid today as when he first thought of it. I wonder how it came to him? Did something happen just then to make him aware of his own body? Did he look down at his hand and suddenly realize the amazing link between mind and body that always fills us with wonder when we become aware of it?

Just as the body is one and has many members ... all the members ... are one body. Look at your own body, he says to the Corinthian Christians. Think of the mystery of it — its limbs, its internal parts, their many functions — yet you are conscious of being one entity, one person. You are many, yet you are one.

So it is with Christ. Now Paul offers another image, another body — the body of Christ. In his mind, and in the minds of his readers, there would have been an image of the body of Jesus that had died for all of them. But Paul points them to the risen and living Christ, and has them — and us — think of all Christians as limbs and members of that body. As he does so, he calls them to consider something that must have stretched their minds to the limit. This body of Christ of which they are a part is wonderfully inclusive, far beyond anything they had envisaged. *We were all baptized into one body — Jews or Greeks, slaves or free.* Twenty centuries later, Paul's image goes on calling us to an inclusiveness that challenges and even disturbs us.

Now Paul begins to work at a thought that is vital to this or any other Christian community. Differences in people do not necessarily mean that they do not belong together. *If the foot would say, "Because I am not a hand I do not belong to the body," that would not make it any less a part of the body.* Sometimes it can be very difficult for a person to see where they can connect with a congregation if that congregation presents a very monochrome identity. Suppose, for instance, that a congregation may have chosen a very charismatic form of worship as its only form. Someone, who for very genuine reasons finds it impossible to worship in such a way, may feel there is no place for him or her in that Christian community. This person may say (echoing the text), "Because I am not a charismatic Christian I do not belong in Saint X's." But Paul points out that this does not make them any less a part of the body. It becomes necessary then for Saint X's to do its utmost to reconsider worship life so that such a person may find an entry point into the community.

Perhaps above all, no member of a Christian community can say to another that he or she does not have some gift to bring to the whole. *The eye cannot say to the hand, "I have no need of you."* Paul's next words reveal the immense sensitivity hidden in his sometimes stern personality. *The members of the body that seem to be weaker are indispensable.* As we follow his argument, it becomes more deeply pastoral. Always taking his images from our own human bodies, he writes, *God has so arranged the body, giving the greater honour to the inferior member.* Here is an echo of something heard again and again in the New Testament. It echoes the song of our Lord's mother: *He has brought down the powerful from their thrones and lifted up the lowly.* It echoes our Lord's insistence that, in the kingdom of God, those we deem to be last will be first.

Notice Paul's reasons for being supportive of varying gifts in a congregation: *that there may be no dissension within the body.* But lack of dissension is not an end in itself. How often a congregation will insist that there be no disagreement in its life, as if total agreement were a mark of Christian community! There can be no life and creativity without some disagreement. For Paul, there is something even more important. Dissension itself is not the danger, but dissension can make it impossible that *members may have the same care for one another.*

Having said all this, Paul shows us how deeply he sees into the nature of Christian community. He sees such a community as an organic whole, a web of being, where *if one member suffers, all suffer together with it; if one member is honoured, all rejoice together with it.* Think of the grace available in such a community to every member, both in their times of need and vulnerability, and in their times of joy.

The Gospel

We will never know whether this passage was already selected for that Sabbath day, or whether our Lord himself chose to turn to it in the scroll. Whatever the case may be, it is a dramatic and significant moment. Although little is known about Jesus, people are already talking about him in Nazareth. Luke has just told us that he began to teach in their synagogues. In view of what happens next, Luke may be speaking ironically when he adds that, to this point, *Jesus was praised by everyone.* Luke may also be signalling something when he tells us that Nazareth was the place where he had been brought up. Home is where we can be most vulnerable and most tested.

Jesus finishes reading the great text of Isaiah. Perhaps it was the wedding of the impressive language of scripture with the natural authority of the reader that caused *the eyes of all in the synagogue [to be] fixed on him.*

From the way Luke describes this scene, we know that he regards it as extremely significant. There is a precision about the images. Jesus *stood up to read, and the scroll … was given to him … He unrolled the scroll and found the place.* When Jesus has finished reading, we see the same vivid images. Jesus *rolled up the scroll, gave it back … and sat down … The eyes of all … were fixed on him. He began to say …* It is as if Luke were insisting that we be fully present, not missing a single nuance of this moment.

Why? Because Jesus' decision to choose this passage indicates how he sees his role at this starting point of his public ministry. He sees himself as *liberator.* It may be that no single word can describe our Lord's ministry, but at this moment, as he stands in the synagogue in Nazareth, there is no doubt about the way in which he sees his role. We hear it in the quiet deliberation of his words: *"Today this scripture has been fulfilled in your hearing."*

As we listen to him read, we hear echoes not only of Isaiah's voice speaking centuries earlier, but of two other voices just before our Lord's birth. One is the voice of his mother singing her song of joy, a song bearing also a note of justice and liberation. She sings of a God who *has lifted up the lowly and has filled the hungry with good things.* The other is the voice of Zechariah, the father of John, Jesus' cousin. Zechariah sings of his hopes for his young son's life. John's role will also be *to bring good news.* He will *give knowledge of salvation.* He will *give light to those who sit in darkness.* He will *guide ... into the way of peace.*

This moment in Nazareth is full of rich associations for our Lord. Probably the voice of his mother often expressed her early hopes for his life. The voice of Isaiah would have spoken to him through the rabbi in the village school.

For us, the greatness of this passage lies in the many levels of meaning in words such as *the poor ... the captives ... the blind.* Sometimes our Lord will reach out to those who are physically poor. At another time he will speak of those who are *poor in spirit.* He will heal those who are physically blind while also condemning those who are spiritually and morally blind. At all levels, our Lord comes to us as liberator. We need to ask what this means for his faithful people in the world of our own time. It is perfectly obvious to others!

Fourth Sunday after the Epiphany: Proper 4

Jeremiah 1:4–10
Psalm 71:1–6
1 Corinthians 13:1–13
Luke 4:21–30

Weavings

In each reading, there is a sense of being called to a vocation that is far from easy. To be faithful to the vocation will require God's grace in the living out of life.

First Reading. Jeremiah realizes that he was destined for his vocation as prophet even before he was born.

The Psalm. The psalmist has committed himself to God but realizes that he will always need God's grace to be faithful.

Second Reading. We are called to the way of love, but since that is the ultimate quality of living, it can be a very stern test of our resolve.

The Gospel. Jesus realizes that he wishes to liberate people from the many prisons they build for themselves, but he also realizes that people can resent the very source of their liberation.

Reflections

First Reading

We can imagine what it must have been like to have been a very young man in that long-ago society. Your country is going through a most difficult period, its social life unstable, its future threatened by great powers. You are idealistic and deeply concerned. You feel you must take some part in the struggle for the future. You are under no illusions that it will be easy, but the advantage of your being young is that you feel you can handle whatever is to come.

All of this sounds within the opening lines of this passage. *The word of the Lord came to me.* Jeremiah is quite certain of his being called. This is no personal illusion or obsession. Notice the language he uses. He hears God as telling him, *I formed you ... I consecrated you ... I appointed you.* There could not be a deeper certainty about one's role in life. We ourselves know the joy and peace that can come in life when we are aware of something calling us, and when we are certain of the validity of the call.

Because we are all human, we know too the moments of panic that can come as we contemplate a task ahead. We hear this in Jeremiah's voice: *"Ah, Lord God! Truly I do not know how to speak, for I am only a boy."* How realistic and honest scripture is, absolutely aware of all the twists and turns of our human nature.

We sometimes know the extraordinary strength that can come from knowing we are in the hands of a will greater and higher than our own. To Jeremiah comes the assurance, *I send you ... I command you.*

Now we hear a distant warning implicit in what Jeremiah hears. *Do not be afraid of them.* There is going to be a *them* that will have to be faced. There is a *them* in every one of our lives, a *them* that will be encountered at every stage in life. There will be many names for *them* — rivals, competitors, opponents, even enemies. For each one of us, the faces of *them* will be different, but the question will always be the same. How do we struggle with *them?* And the answer is always the same for the man or woman who trusts in a faithful God: *I am with you to deliver you, says the Lord.*

One thing the Bible teaches us again and again — the power of human speech. *The Lord ... touched my mouth. The Lord said ... I have put my words in your mouth.* We need to remember this when we speak in certain circumstances, especially when we risk not being in control of the words we instinctively may say. There will be times when we want to hurt — perhaps because we ourselves have been hurt — or to return an insulting remark, or to explode with impatience. At such times we need to remember that God has indeed touched our mouths, and we need to search for a word other than the ones our feelings dictate, the word that God has placed there. By the same token, there will be opportunities to say a longed-for word of comfort or encouragement or guidance, a word that can have a great effect on another's life. Then too, we need to make a silent prayer to say the word that God wishes our mouth to speak.

The Psalm

In these verses we learn again a paradox about ourselves. We are a life-long mingling of strength and weakness, confidence and uncertainty, resilience and fragility. To trust in God is to have a sense of security, of *refuge.* At the same time, I am never free of the need for that security and refuge. I may look to God as *my strong rock ... castle ... crag ... stronghold,* but I am seldom free from the many threats around me and within me that never cease oppressing. My life is a rhythm of doing battle with many things, using all my strengths and gifts to prevail. Yet I am strongest when I realize that I am not alone and have never been alone. That which gives me *confidence*, that by which *I have been sustained,* that which has always *been my strength,* issues not from myself but from the One who has formed me.

Second Reading

Paul has just listed many gifts that we need in order to serve our Lord. Each one of us cannot have them all. The gifts of God, infinitely varied, are dispersed among us. When we gather as a community, these gifts are waiting to emerge to make the community rich and strong.

Having said all this, Paul pauses to take breath. Of course, we cannot know that he actually paused, but I strongly suspect that he did. First he says, *Strive for the greater gifts.* He doesn't specifically mention which gifts are greater. He seems to be stepping up a level from the *gifts.* Now he steps even beyond what he thinks are the *greater gifts.* He is ready to show us a gift beyond even the greater gifts. Here is the ultimate gift. *I will show you a still more excellent way* (12:31).

The way is nothing less than the way of love. Nothing can approach it; nothing can be a substitute for it. Paul has listed other gifts that are necessary and worthy. But he startles us with a reminder that every one of these gifts can co-exist in us with a shocking lack of love. His first example is particularly sobering. Paul points out that receiving the gift of the Holy Spirit, even to the point of finding oneself speaking in tongues, does not guarantee that we will become a loving spirit! Great powers of insight *(prophetic powers),* great intellectual powers *(mysteries and knowledge),* the strongest faith imaginable *(to remove mountains),* even acts of great self-sacrifice, can all be accompanied by a ghastly lovelessness!

As Paul begins to list the properties of love, we begin to realize the limits of our human capacity to love fully! Is our love for someone always patient and kind? Are we never boastful or envious or arrogant or rude? Do we never insist on our own way? Are we never irritable or resentful? All of us know the answers to these questions only too well.

Does our love endure all things? Not always. Does human love end? Yes, frequently and sometimes tragically? So what is Paul talking about? *Love* in this passage means ultimate love, the source of love, God's love — the quality of love lived out for us in our Lord. When we realize this, every statement about love falls into place and makes sense. This love is paramount. Before this love, all our knowledge and all our prophecy — could we translate prophecy as insight? — bow down.

The whole of our lives is our attempting to grow towards this love. Everything about us is incomplete; everything we do is partial. Our deepest insights are of a reality only dimly grasped. When we do grasp the reality of God's love, we will find that it is grasping us! We will know fully, but only at the price of being ourselves fully known. We will understand what it means to love fully, only when we have come to realize that we ourselves are fully loved.

I suspect that this passage is the most autobiographical of all Paul's writings. We watch him baring himself to others as he acknowledges the yawning gulf between his best efforts to love and be loved, and the ultimate love that met him on the Damascus Road and captured him there.

The Gospel

When we enter this scene, the atmosphere is full of excitement. Nothing untoward has yet happened. After reading the Isaiah passage but before putting away the scroll, Jesus makes a simple short statement: *"Today this scripture has been fulfilled in your hearing."* One cannot help wondering if he meant to say more at this point but had to stop because of the explosive response from the congregation. They were amazed! There is something impressive and intriguing about this local boy, newly returned among them. *"Is not this Joseph's son?"* someone asks; and this question is probably on many lips. So far, they seem not to resent his statement about the passage being fulfilled in their hearing. There was no reason to hear it as a personal claim. It could well have been a reference to the ongoing work of God in society.

Now Jesus' tone changes. Is there a hint of weary sarcasm? *Doubtless you will quote to me this proverb, "Doctor, cure yourself! Do here also in your home town the things we have heard you did at Capernaum."* Why does he say this? Have people already said things to him on this visit home that we have not overheard? Has he heard things said in the street? It sounds as if he has been hurt to some extent and feels resentful. Otherwise, why do we hear the bitter remark, *"No prophet is accepted in the prophet's home town"?*

As if a flood of pent-up feelings has been released in Jesus, he now seems to goad the crowd. The two examples he gives are almost certain to have an adverse reaction. *"Elijah was sent to none [of the widows in Israel] except to a widow ... in Sidon."* Significantly, this widow was not a Jew. Again, *"None [of the lepers in Israel] was cleansed except Naaman the Syrian."* And again, Naaman was not a Jew.

Every word is meant to sting the listening ears in the synagogue — the God of Israel deliberately neglecting his own people to serve and heal foreigners! The place erupts in anger. Jesus is swept up in the crowd. There are death threats — very real considering where they take him. Probably only his natural authority, and the real fear of Roman retaliation, saved him. He leaves Nazareth. Today, this passage warns against our having a limited vision of God. In contrast to our own often grudging and limited commitments, Our Lord pledges his utter commitment to the work of liberating human lives. If we are not prepared to offer ourselves as the instruments of God's work, then others will be chosen.

Fifth Sunday after the Epiphany: Proper 5

Isaiah 6:1–8 (9–13)
Psalm 138
1 Corinthians 15:1–11
Luke 5:1–11

Weavings

Each of the readings points in some way to those moments when we become aware of the mysterious presence of God in our experience.

First Reading. Faced with a major change in his responsibilities, Isaiah enters the temple to reflect on the meaning of events in his life. In doing so, he is given a vision of God that becomes his vocation.

The Psalm. Because God has responded to him in the past, the psalmist believes that God responds to human need when called upon.

Second Reading. Paul points to the many people who have experienced the presence of God in the risen Christ. He ends the list with his own claim to such an experience.

The Gospel. In a moment of his working day as a fisherman, Peter becomes aware of Jesus in a new and piercing way that is both disturbing and deeply captivating.

Reflections

First Reading

Isaiah's experience is very much ours. He comes to an intense sense of God's presence *in the year that King Uzziah died.* Our culture is experiencing a return to the spiritual dimension of life at a time when many "kings" — many sources of authority and tradition — are dying and changing.

For Isaiah, God is *high and lofty.* For us, Christian experience has become, in a certain sense, heightened. On the whole, Christian faith is more intense. That intensity can show in anger and anxiety and fear, or it can be experienced as a renewal of a joyous and hopeful faith. There are many movements of the Spirit among Christians. Some such movements are wholesome and responsible, others can become power seeking and irresponsible. For Isaiah, *the pivots on the thresholds shook.* There is a sense of foundations shifting beneath us. For Isaiah, *the house filled with smoke.* No single clear road lies before us into the future.

This passage gives us a great pastoral gift. It shows us someone who in many ways is a spiritual giant, yet who is still unable to say "yes" to the call of God when first called! This should be comforting, because most of us are not always over-ready with a fervent and immediate "yes" to the call of God!

By looking closely, we see that Isaiah does not exactly refuse the first call. He becomes aware of the presence of God. He feels deeply disturbed. Then there sweeps over him a sense of utter inadequacy. It is a feeling we all know very well. *I am lost. I am a man of unclean lips.* He feels equally despairing about the society he lives in — again a very common experience these days. *I live among a people of unclean lips.*

Notice what happens now. The little word *yet* makes the difference. Isaiah feels that neither he nor his society has anything to offer God. Yet he cannot completely walk away from this presence that he feels sure is nothing less than God. *Yet my eyes have seen the King, the Lord of hosts.* He feels held in what we might call today the force-field of God's presence. In this moment of hesitation, the grace of God is given. Isaiah is touched by the fire of grace. He is enabled to see himself differently. *Your guilt has departed.* His sense of inadequacy is summarily dealt with. It is not so much that he is or is not inadequate to respond to God. We are all inadequate in some ways. But something tells Isaiah, and each one of us, that our inadequacy is accepted and can be used for God's purposes. We are enabled to offer ourselves without a sense of shame. *Here am I* — just as I am, adequate or inadequate — *send me!*

The Psalm

As we overhear the psalmist praising God, we might easily miss a small phrase. *"Before the gods I sing your praise,"* he says. He is telling us, of course, not that he praises the God of Israel while standing in front of lesser gods, but that he chooses the God of Israel before and above such lesser gods.

We are being given a valuable piece of spiritual direction. Within each of us, there are many lesser gods vying for attention. Each of them pulls us towards itself. There is the god of our fears, the god of our anxieties, the god of our lusts, the god of our demanding self. The psalmist knows these gods, as do we all. And he will not, nor should we, allow them to come before God.

There is a significant spiritual insight here. The lesser gods do their very best to come before God, to stand between God and ourselves. They make urgent and incessant claims. And we must make conscious efforts to force them aside. The exercise of our spirituality is in the most literal sense an exercising, a deliberate activity that we must constantly pursue. Notice the active verbs of the psalm: *I will give you thanks, O Lord ... sing your praise ... bow down.*

Most important in my relationship with God is to acknowledge my self-insufficiency. To do so is to begin to reach out for a source of sufficiency beyond myself. *Though the Lord be high, he cares for the lowly. When I called, you answered me. You increased my strength within me.* The important thing is that I must first "call."

Second Reading

Paul is nearing the end of the most difficult letter he has written to any Christian community. He has had to be very stern with the Corinthians. But at this point, the sternness has shifted to encouragement. This scripture rings with joyous affirmation. It brings *good news.* The passage sets out what Paul deems to be *of first importance* for a Christian. Since we are doing much searching and casting around these days in our efforts to define Christian faith, we should look carefully at this passage. For Paul, it is of first importance *that Christ died for our sins ... that he was buried ... that he was raised ... and that he appeared.* Here is the very heart of Christian faith.

The last of these short statements — short and simple but massive in their significance — is particularly important for us today. In recent years we have become greatly exercised about the person of Jesus, about his death and its significance for our lives, and about the utterly mysterious event that we call resurrection. We need to be very clear that the endless flood of paperbacks available to us will not alone solve our questions. This is not to say we shouldn't read them. We will learn much from many of them. But we most certainly will not find some neat and precise proof of our Lord's resurrection. This is not a problem to which, if we search long enough, we can find a solution.

Knowing that our Lord is risen does not come as the solution to a problem or the answer to a question. Paul tells us that it is given to us by grace. He is so anxious for us to realize this, that he uses the word *grace* like a mantra. *By the grace of God I am what I am, and his grace toward me has not been in vain ... It was not I but the grace of God that is with me.* For Paul, this grace lies in the fact that the risen Lord has appeared to him. Paul is aware that the risen Christ has appeared to many others. He lists some instances for us. *To Cephas, then to the twelve. Then he appeared to more than five hundred brothers and sisters ... Then he appeared to James, then to all the apostles.* But of paramount importance for Paul is that *he appeared also to me.*

There is a kind of trap that ensnares many Christians. Because we know the devastating way our Lord appeared to Paul, we tend to assume that, unless an equally shattering Damascus Road experience happens to us, we, as very ordinary and unworthy Christians, have not encountered our risen Lord. Nothing could be further from the truth. Paul himself insists that in terms of worthiness he stands in last place! He emphasizes this and agonizes about it. *Last of all, as to one untimely born, he appeared also to me. For I am the least of the apostles, unfit to be called an apostle.* We may not have persecuted the church of God, but we certainly have let it down many times, and have been unworthy of our membership in it. We don't even need to be told this. In this sense, everything Paul says about himself is true of us: *last of all ... least of all ... unfit.*

So we have established one thing clearly. Encounters with the risen Lord are neither earned nor deserved. They are gifts of God's grace to us. We need to ask ourselves why we are seeking to encounter our Lord. What do we want of him? What need within us sends us in search for him? In truth, this very searching is, of itself, his rising and walking in the landscape of our soul. The questing for him can mark the beginning of his rising. It is not that we must desperately look for an imagined correct Damascus Road that, when travelled, will bring us to some tempestuous encounter. We are already on our Damascus Road, and beside us there already walks the stranger who waits for us to engage him.

This is the *good news that I [Paul] proclaimed to you, which you in turn received, in which also you stand, through which also you are being saved.* Notice this last statement. You and I are *being saved.* We are experiencing a process. We are on a journey. Christian life can indeed have its special and even shatteringly wonderful experiences of the presence of our Lord, but these are not the "be all and end all" of Christian life. Such experiences are given so that the questing of our life can go on.

The Gospel

One can easily imagine how the small indentations along the shore of the lake could have become natural gathering places. The area slopes slightly toward the edge of the water. The rising ground behind provides an echo chamber for the voice. Our Lord apparently prefers to speak from a slight distance. The few yards of water between him and the crowd may help to carry his words more clearly.

After Jesus has spoken to the crowd, we move into significant things. For some reason, Jesus suggests dropping the nets. It diminishes the episode in no way to suggest that he may have noticed some movement of fish from his position slightly higher on the shore. Peter points out that a whole night's fishing has produced nothing. Significance comes in the words, *"Yet, if you say so."* Here is trust and respect from disciple to master. Perhaps this is not the first time that following instructions has paid off!

But this time the result is startling. So much is caught that they have to call for help. They cannot believe their eyes. Suddenly Peter senses that there is more here than meets his or anyone else's eye. He becomes aware of something for which he has no language. His mind may have played with terms such as power or presence — something more than human. But no neat defining language will come; so he gives expression to his reaction in a more instinctive way. He kneels in the boat. It must have been difficult, clumsy, undignified. Then the truth comes from the depths of Peter's being. He is aware that he is in the presence of something other than his own limited and guilt-ridden humanity: *"Go away from me Lord, for I am a sinful man!"*

If we are fortunate, we have all done this kind of kneeling — perhaps before an act of supreme courage, a scene of great beauty, a person of immense spiritual stature, a work of supreme art. We have done this kind of kneeling in the moment when an act of worship, familiar and oft repeated, has suddenly catapulted us unawares to unexpected heights, leaving us quietly weeping, not knowing why. Or should we say — knowing why, yet having no language to state why? One is aware only of Presence, before whom there is nothing to do but bow down, knowing that every conceivable aspect of one's being is transparent to this Presence, is being judged by this Presence, yet that even the judgement will be loving. At such moments, there is an awareness of vast plenitude in the soul, the plenitude that Peter's eyes saw in the silver leaping of the fish yet his whole being recognized as something more than fish. There is a beautiful Gaelic song that prays, *"Ag Criost an mhuir — in liontaibh De go gasthar sinn"* (By the Christ of the sea may we be caught in the nets of God).

Sixth Sunday after the Epiphany: Proper 6

Jeremiah 17:5–10
Psalm 1
1 Corinthians 15:12–20
Luke 6:17–26

Weavings

In all of these readings, there is a warning about not acknowledging our need for God's grace.

First Reading. Jeremiah is hammering at his people's continual temptation to assume that they can achieve everything by their own efforts.

The Psalm. The psalmist emphasizes that virtue lies in turning to God as the resource for our lives.

Second Reading. Paul could not be more specific in his insistence that belief in our Lord's resurrection is the heart of Christian faith.

The Gospel. Our Lord presents us with a vision of life as it would be if it were lived in and for the kingdom of God. This vision is challenging us to reconsider everything we wish to preserve in our lives.

Reflections

First Reading

Cursed are those who trust in mere mortals and make mere flesh their strength. When we hear this theme expressed in scripture — and it often is — we need to avoid interpreting it as a negative view of human nature and capability. Jeremiah is not dismissing the abilities and strengths of his people. The words *mere mortals ... mere flesh* are not a sneer at humanity. They are more a burst of exasperation from a person who is desperately anxious that his people see something to which they are blind. Jeremiah is saying something like this — if only you will be prepared to reach out for the grace and guidance of God, your own human abilities will be blessed and strengthened in every way! In other words, instead of denigrating people, he is in a sense complementing them. How great you could be, he seems to say, if only you linked your human gifts to God's grace!

Jeremiah's insight is as true for us as it was for long-ago Israel. People often think that Christian faith is nothing more than dependency. We can't handle life ourselves; so we invent a source called God to do it for us. Nothing could be further from the truth. Life has to be lived by each one of us. This is why we were given various gifts and resources within ourselves and among ourselves in our relationships. But millions of Christians — and other believers in God — have come to realize that, when we turn beyond ourselves for grace, we receive grace!

Hearts [who] turn away from the Lord ... shall be like a shrub in the desert. This image comes from the terrain that Jeremiah lived in. There is all the difference in the world between a tree struggling to survive in the desert and a tree growing near water. It is not that a tree in the desert is any less fine or worthy than one by water. But a desert tree must put every atom of its energy into mere survival, because it has almost no resources beyond itself. If it had such outside resources, it would probably be just as magnificent as a tree that can draw from a nearby water source. *Those who trust in the Lord ... shall be like a tree planted by water.*

Something very simple yet absolutely essential is being said to us here. We will be the richer for reaching out for God's grace. Jeremiah first says, *Blessed are those who trust in the Lord.* Then he alters his words slightly to say something important that we might easily miss. *Blessed are those whose trust is the Lord.* He seems to be suggesting that the ability to trust is itself the presence of God in our lives. We know the lovely phrase that forms the basis of a beautiful Taizé chant. *"Ubi Caritas, ibi Deus est"* (Where love is, there is God), it sings. In a similar way, Jeremiah is saying to us that where trust exists, there in that trust is God.

Notice what Jeremiah says are the consequences of a tree being near water. *When heat comes ... its leaves shall stay green ... In drought ... it does not cease to bear fruit.* We can see immediately the parallels to human experience. To possess a source of grace beyond ourselves is to have a greater chance of coming through those times when life can seem to be a desert of pain or loneliness or anxiety, to name only a few experiences.

The Psalm

The text of the psalm is a clear and immediate echo of the reading. Once again we are being shown two images of the land. We walk past *trees planted by streams of water,* and then suddenly we must bend forward and guard our eyes and faces from the sting of *chaff which the wind drives away.*

I often think that these utterly contrasting images are natural to a writer who lives in a very small country. In Israel, it is only a short distance from desert to oasis, or from bare brown hills to plains and valleys of waving grass or corn. One is constantly made aware of the varied tapestry of physical geography. Consequently, the varied tapestry of psychological geography

— human character and experience — also comes to mind. Once again, the trees and the chaff stand for choices we all make in life. What course do we choose to follow? What companions do we choose for the journey? *Happy are they who have not walked in the counsel of the wicked.*

What is essential in life? Nowadays we are fond of using the term *centred.* We speak of looking for a centre. The psalm is responding to this search, but it says that we make a mistake if we think that we will find the centre in our own selves. This point is easy to miss, because of the language of the psalmist. When he says, *Happy are they [whose] ... delight is in the law of the Lord,* he is suggesting that the centre we seek lies beyond ourselves. This does not mean that we should not examine ourselves. It does not mean that we cannot plumb the depths of our souls, as we do our searching. But it is telling us that, at the end of all our striving and journeying, the discovery that the centre for the self lies within God will satisfy that same self more than anything else. Just as a tree takes its life from the water outside itself, so we are born to draw life from God. Just as the water enables such trees to bear *fruit in due season,* so our decision to draw energy and inspiration for our lives from God will enable us to live creatively and effectively in the world.

Second Reading

How can some of you say there is no resurrection of the dead? As we listen to today's voices arguing about our Lord's resurrection, searching for language to express our groping understandings, it is almost reassuring to discover that the resurrection was an issue for doubt and dispute in the first generation of the church's life. Even the line of reasoning expressed by the Corinthian voices sounds quite modern. They are saying, in effect, "There is no such thing as the resurrection of the dead; therefore, it cannot be that Jesus has been raised from the dead."

As with a great many people today, Paul's readers in Corinth fall into the trap of interpreting resurrection as resuscitation. It is clear from this great passage of Paul — and clearer as we read on in this chapter — that he is thinking of a reality beyond mere resuscitation of the body that Jesus knew for thirty-odd years and that you and I know as the vessel of our own being. The Christian claim, which Paul puts to his readers and to us, is that the Lord who appeared among his friends had moved beyond death into a mode of being where he was no longer a prisoner of time and space, as we are. By saying this, we are not trying to make it easier to believe in the risen Christ. No matter in what terms we express the fact of his being risen, it remains an awe-inspiring mystery, and will never be understood as we in our culture wish to understand before accepting something as true.

Notice how Paul responds to what is being said in the community. He does not browbeat or argue people into submission. Instead, he asks them to consider the consequences for themselves, and for their faith, if they truly decide that Christ is *not* risen. *If for this life only we have hoped in Christ, we are of all people most to be pitied.* It is not enough to regard Jesus as a wonderful example of how life is lived, an example we should then emulate. Paul makes it impossible for us to play games with who or what Jesus was — Jesus the great teacher, Jesus the guru, Jesus the wonderful storyteller. Paul sees Jesus as moving our human nature, the human nature he fully shared, beyond the prison of sin and death where we live out this same human nature, into the presence of the Divine where our humanity is accepted and forgiven through Jesus Christ our Lord. In a sense, Christ leads the way for us. He becomes *the first fruits of those who have died.* Hence, our use of these very words — through Jesus Christ our Lord — whenever we approach the presence of God in prayer.

The Gospel

He came down with them and stood on a level place. The reference is intriguing. One wants to know where this level place was and where he came down from. North of the lake is usually called upper Galilee. We know that Jesus has just chosen the twelve from among a larger group of disciples. He may have done this somewhere in the higher country above the lake, and then come down. Because the crowd contained people from *Judea, Jerusalem, and the coast of Tyre and Sidon,* we probably are meeting him somewhere on the level area near the north shore of the lake. This area would be reasonably central to those places.

They had come to hear him and to be healed of their diseases. One wonders if there is a little sadness here. We have hints that Jesus realized how many crowded around him for the satisfying of personal need rather than for any spiritual hunger or any wish to hear what he had to say. Luke says that *all in the crowd were trying to touch him, for power came out of him and healed all of them.* We need not assume that all these healings are physical. Jesus is an extremely charismatic person whose very presence exudes peace and healing. I would suggest that this is one sense in which Luke speaks of Jesus as having *healed all of them.*

Now comes an intriguing phrase. Luke tells us that Jesus *looked up at his disciples* as he began to speak. If he were about to speak to the surrounding crowd, it is strange that he pointedly focused on the disciples. But since he has just chosen these particular followers, it is natural that his words would be directed especially towards them. It is as if our Lord is saying, "You have decided to commit yourself to me. Now let me try to get you to understand what you have accepted." If this is indeed true, then these disciples receive a most sobering description of their own future, should they remain loyal to Jesus and his vision. He must have turned their world upside down, and unless we hear this passage as turning our own world upside down, then we are not really hearing it!

In these next few moments, Jesus takes what it means to be poor and what it means to be rich and reverses all the categories! In this sense, he turns everybody's world upside down! *Blessed are you who are poor ... who are hungry ... who weep ... Blessed are you when people hate you ... exclude ... revile ... defame you. Woe to you who are rich ... who are full ... you will be hungry ... you will mourn and weep.*

Try to imagine what it was like to hear this for the first time. We hear it now with all the deadening familiarity of a lifetime's listening, but we can be certain that almost no one hearing this for the first time could take it in. When occasionally these words do explode in the ears of a particular person, they transform his or her life and bring into being a person whom the rest of us regard with a kind of awe, the awe that we reserve for the spiritual giants called saints, either in past or present times. In this sense, these words of Jesus are dangerous. They contain a vision of reality that challenges every aspect of what goes on in human life and human society. They reveal something so novel that we even refer to it — as our Lord did — as being a different realm, a different kingdom, *the kingdom of God.*

Perhaps the most piercing insight of this passage is given to us by a voice from our own twentieth century. In many ways, Dietrich Bonhoeffer embodied the values of the kingdom of God as he challenged the values of the terrible kingdom of Nazi Germany. Bonhoeffer once said that, when Jesus Christ calls a person, he calls that person to die. At the heart of this passage we have read today, Jesus is saying this to the new disciples. They would have to become nothing less than a new kind of human being. One cannot help wondering what their thoughts were as they pondered their first day of discipleship. What are our thoughts as we try to relate to this terrifying passage?

Seventh Sunday after the Epiphany: Proper 7

Genesis 45:3–11, 15
Psalm 37:1–12, 41–42
1 Corinthians 15:35–38, 42–50
Luke 6:27–38

Weavings

One of the great triumphs of the human spirit is to remain "sweet" in the face of adversity or enmity. To rise above such adversity without bitterness is in itself a kind of resurrection.

First Reading. After many years, Joseph meets the brothers who once sold him into slavery. He displays immense generosity.

The Psalm. The psalmist tells those who will listen that it is wise not to let the attitudes and behaviour of others dictate one's own attitude to life.

Second Reading. Paul continues to grapple with the mystery of resurrection and how it can be expressed.

The Gospel. Jesus indicates the immeasurable advantages to be gained by refusing to respond to others in terms of judgement and enmity.

Reflections

First Reading

Even in his very first words, we hear the generosity of spirit that Joseph will display more and more as we read on: *"I am Joseph. Is my father still alive?"* Most important for him is to know whether his beloved father is still alive, not to make a dramatic self-presentation to his brothers.

Obviously the brothers are flabbergasted, not because they believe what this man has just said but because they are terrified of another bizarre trap. Joseph has to entice them even to come near him. *Come closer to me.* It is a beautiful statement because it has more than one level of meaning. After the gulf of the intervening years, Joseph genuinely wishes to be emotionally closer to these people. He has every reason to wish to distance himself from them, but he chooses otherwise. Later he will invite them to be physically closer to him by coming to live in Egypt.

"I am your brother Joseph, whom you sold into Egypt." He names the truth in all its ugliness. Perhaps this old story is hinting that, in order to deal with painful things, we need to name them clearly and bluntly. Seeing the shock and fear on the faces before him, Joseph quickly reassures them by describing his own feelings. He is quite certain that everything has happened for a purpose: *"God sent me before you to preserve life."* Joseph sees his own life as emerging from the purpose of a loving God. Even by selling Joseph into slavery, the brothers were unknowingly the agents of the purposes of this same God: *"It was not you who sent me here, but God."* No less than three times he repeats the statement: *God sent me before you.* He is emphasizing that there is nothing negative in this situation, only positive results.

Now we hear wave after wave of generosity issuing from Joseph. *"Come down to me, make no delay! You shall settle in the land of Goshen ... I will provide for you there."* And a lovely thing emerges. Joseph is already a great man, in the sense of his high place and great power in Egypt. We see now that he is also a great human being, a great and generous spirit. Furthermore, this greatness of spirit springs from his view of life. For Joseph, God is the source of life. The purposes of our lives spring from God, and when we believe this, grace also springs from God, enabling us to live out those deep purposes and to remain truly healthy and alive in spirit.

A small thing, but important — Joseph *kissed all his brothers and wept upon them; and after that his brothers talked with him.* The ancient storyteller wants us to understand the importance of actions and gestures, as well as words. Only after there has been an actual physical encounter are the brothers able to talk with Joseph. How important a touch can be, a handshake, a hug, even the simple gesture of a hand on a shoulder. Barriers tumble and encounter takes place.

The Psalm

One of the annoying things in life is that, at least in the short run, it can pay quite handsomely to be unscrupulous. There are many other questionable behaviours that can, for a while, pay off rather well. Playing the power game in various ways, not caring about people who get in the way, fiddling certain accounts. Such practices can produce many pleasant things we would all like to have.

This last admission is important, because the prospering of the unscrupulous becomes doubly annoying when we cannot help but envy the results of their wrongdoing. The psalmist is wise to this little secret about most of us, and he expresses it more than once. *"Do not fret,"* we are advised no less than three times, precisely because we do indulge in a great deal of fretting about the injustices of life. We get angry, and if we are prepared to be honest with ourselves, we know that our anger arises not purely from the other person's unscrupulous methods so much as from our envy of their success. *"Do not fret yourself over the one who prospers,"* we are told. *"Refrain from anger, leave rage alone."* Very good advice — because there is nothing more useless than anger born of envy.

Again, if we are really honest, the alternative suggested by the psalmist does not really excite us. The heart of his message is that *the wicked shall soon wither like the grass.* In our cynical moments, we find this less than persuasive. However, in the long haul of life — which is exactly what the psalmist is getting at — we may come to know and savour the truth of his words: *Those who wait upon the Lord shall possess the land.* This may not be true in a literal sense, but it may be true of the inner land, the country of our own soul and our integrity. One of the salutary consequences of being a Christian is our belief that not only will we have to make peace with the way we have lived, but we will have to answer to one greater than ourselves.

Second Reading

Perhaps we should be more alert to moments of possible humour — intended or otherwise — in scripture. I am tempted to ask, Are you not glad you are not the "someone" in *Someone will ask, "How are the dead raised up?"* Paul has obviously never heard the well-known reassuring statement that there is no such thing as a stupid question! The response to this question is a single thundering word — *fool!*

Maybe this intense response arises out of the seriousness of the subject. Paul is anxious that people grasp what he is trying to say. I suspect that he realized the difficulty people were going to have with the mystery of our Lord's risen presence and life. This has been true in every Christian generation, and it always has — and probably always will — centre around the nature of the human body and the purposes of God for it. This is what Paul now tackles.

What is sown is perishable. Right up front, Paul faces the brutal reality of death as we experience and see it. Notice, however, that he immediately balances this blow with the beauty and hope of the statement, *What is raised is imperishable.* Here is a lesson for everyone having to say difficult things. Paul continues his sensitive balancing of the harsh with the hopeful. *Sown in dishonour ... raised in glory. Physical body ... spiritual body. Man of dust ... man of heaven.* He then climaxes his explanation with the categorical statement that *flesh and blood cannot inherit the kingdom of God.* These words should make it perfectly clear to us that, when we speak of the resurrection of our Lord, we are not speaking about the resuscitation of the body that died on the cross.

As he wrestles with this mystery, Paul reaches back to Genesis to express a wonderful insight. *"The first man, Adam, became a living being,"* he tells us. *The last Adam [referring to Jesus] became a life-giving spirit.* I have always felt that these are among the most significant words ever said about our Lord. For me they represent the nearest expression we can find of what happened when our Lord moved through death. When I use the words, "moved through death," I am not in any way diminishing the reality of his death. Jesus died. This truth is central to Christian faith. But unless we are prepared to dismiss the cumulative evidence of scripture, the report of his earliest followers, and the witness of countless Christians in subsequent generations, Jesus becomes a source of incalculable spiritual power to those who are prepared to extend their trust in him beyond the barrier of death. He becomes — and note that we are not merely saying that he became — what Paul describes as *a life-giving spirit.*

I find that the phrase, *a life-giving spirit,* echoes in my mind and wishes to say more to me. It seems to be asking me how I can, as a follower of this life-giving spirit, become myself a spirit that gives life to others. If my vocation as a Christian is to become like my Lord, then an element of my vocation must be to emulate him in this — that I endeavour, to the extent I can, to give life to others. I then have to ask myself what this might mean. I think it means being a person from whom the creative things of life flow towards others, instead of those things that deaden and shadow human experience. I would suggest that *hope* is life-giving, also forgiveness, acceptance, openness, understanding, encouragement. Above all, the vast and mysterious thing we call *love.* Because I am all too human, I will naturally sometimes fail to be life-giving to others. There will be times when I shall be weak and vulnerable, and will seek others to be life-giving to me. But in so far as my human condition allows, it seems to me that my vocation is to be *a life-giving spirit.*

The Gospel

Once again, as I read this passage, I cannot help recalling how Luke opens this episode in our Lord's ministry. You may recall Luke telling us that Jesus, even though there was a great crowd, *looked up at his disciples* (v. 20 in this chapter). Again, you may recall that he has just selected them to be his special followers (v. 13). I see our Lord speaking to the crowd but looking particularly at this small group on whom the future now depends. I suggest that, by looking towards them in this special way, he may be communicating to them something like the following: "All these people around us hear me saying these things, but it is highly unlikely that most of them will either comprehend or put into practice what I am saying. Therefore, I look to you to begin at least to understand and to realize that this is the vision I offer you, and that this is the price you will pay for becoming part of my vision."

And so our Lord continues to disclose the vision of the kingdom we know so well, but which remains forever beyond our grasp. *Love your enemies ... bless those who curse you ... pray for those who abuse you ... offer the other cheek ... give to everyone.* In some sense, these are words of terror in what they demand of us. Even as we listen to them, we begin to look for ways out, for some reasonable compromises in the face of these utterly unreasonable — in terms of our world — demands. But even as we do this, Jesus goes on to deprive us of any possible compromises. So we think we are reasonably loving men and women? Jesus shatters this illusion by saying, *"If you love those who love you, what credit is that to you?"* So we think of ourselves as reasonably generous? Jesus shatters this by saying, *"If you do good to those who do good to you, what credit is that to you?"*

I said that this kingdom remains forever beyond our grasp. Not totally, of course. There are great souls who grasp its glory for a moment. Some act of sublime self-sacrifice, some gesture of immense generosity with no hope of recompense — and for a fleeting moment the kingdom is embodied in the world. Heaven and earth are for a moment bridged.

And what is the basis for these terrifying claims? It is expressed in one succinct statement: *Your reward will be great, and you will be children of the Most High; for he is kind to the ungrateful and the wicked.* And who are the unkind and the wicked? Each one of us! We are astounded. Me unkind? Me wicked? And the quiet answer is "yes," in terms of the kingdom of God! And while we try to comprehend what this means, our Lord offers us a great truth about life here on earth, whatever we may learn about life in his kingdom. Here on earth one thing is sure: *The measure you give will be the measure you get back.*

Eighth Sunday after the Epiphany: Proper 8

Isaiah 55:10–13
Psalm 92:1–4, 11–14
1 Corinthians 15:51–58
Luke 6:39–49

Weavings

The readings tell us of different moments and ways of God's creative action in our lives.

First Reading. Just as God brings forth life in the activities of nature, so God's purpose emerges in specific events.

The Psalm. The certainty that faithfulness to God gives life its greatest meaning brings a burst of praise from the psalmist.

Second Reading. Paul drives home his assurance that what gives meaning and purpose to our lives is the hope of eternal life.

The Gospel. Jesus speaks of the absolute necessity for us to realize that transformation must begin within ourselves, and of the great transformation possible when we choose him as the foundation of our lives.

Reflections

First Reading

As we listen to the prophet, we hear many rich nuances in his words, nuances we have tended to forget in our more urban and northern world. Notice the precise sequence he carefully spells out, as if he is seeing it all vividly as he speaks. First *the rain and the snow,* then a time of waiting: *they do not return there until* ... Now the time to *bring forth and sprout,* then the time for *seed to the sower,* and at last *bread to the eater.*

Every stage of the seasonal sequence is seen as beyond our control, the action of a creating God. Human life is essentially dependent. These days we rarely remember that, in company with all life on this planet, we are totally dependent on this natural cycle of environmental change. The sequence that begins with *rain* and ends with *bread* has only to become unbalanced to a minor degree, and we are in deep trouble.

Isaiah then extrapolates from nature and points to the same immense power operating in all the purposes of God. In this case, he points to the activity of God in history, trying to get his people to see how God's actions open great possibilities for their future. *You shall go out in joy, and be led back in peace.* The same burst of growth and beauty that they see in nature is also manifesting in their own situation — they are a people liberated and led homeward. *The mountains ... shall burst into song. Instead of the briar shall come up the myrtle.*

This passage seems to be telling us that we need to recover a sense of history as somehow the domain of God's activity. I say "somehow," because this view is problematical. Is everything that happens in history of God? One would hope not, considering some of the terrible things that go on. The Bible helps us out of this dilemma. Time and history, from a biblical point of view, are seen as the ground of conflict between God and the powers of evil. Therefore, we can at no time point with certainty to a particular event and say that it is or is not according to the purpose of God.

However, we can regard time and history as a ground where the purpose of God is present in the conflict and, we trust, will finally triumph. This alone is sufficient basis for Christian hope. It allows us to see time and history as more than merely an infinitely complex interaction of countless events and forces, all driven by the clash of differing human wills and purposes. Using the language of the prophet, in time and history there will always be both the thorn and the cypress, both the brier and the myrtle. We hope, with Isaiah, that *instead of the thorn shall come up the cypress; instead of the brier shall come up the myrtle.*

The Psalm

As I read this psalm, I am also hearing the moods and feelings of two great songs from the world of the American musical. One is the song from *My Fair Lady* and the other from *South Pacific.* The first is sung by Eliza Doolittle as soon as she is alone after her initial outing with Henry Higgins. "I could have danced all night," she sings again and again. The second song is sung by Nellie Forbush when she realizes that her relationship with Emile de Beque has become a love affair. She almost leaps on to the stage to sing, "I'm in love! I'm in love with a wonderful guy!"

If we can accord the psalmist a stage entry, he too seems to leap among us. *It is a good thing to give thanks to the Lord ... to sing praises to your name ... tell of your loving-kindness ... your faithfulness!* The phrases tumble over one another as if he cannot get them out fast enough. *You have made me glad ... I shout for joy!* Nothing else matters at this moment. There is not a single shadow on the horizon. In his present euphoria, everything shrinks in size before the greatness of the Lord. *The Lord is my rock.*

Such moments as this come to all of us from time to time. We think of them as "highs." We realize that they cannot last long, because we cannot stay high. But such moments are valuable. They can be an opportunity to escape from what the psalmist in other songs calls the *pit*. Sometimes a high can lift us out of the prison of the self and enable us to reach beyond ourselves, into the realm of the heart and the soul, where God waits to be discovered and to offer us more than our limited selves. This can be especially true if we are prepared to see such moments of joy as themselves the gift of a loving God.

As modern people, we are often only too ready with glib and small interpretations of our feelings. We will say sometimes that a moment of unexplained joy is "just" an adrenaline rush, or "just" a chemical change, or "just" a psychological process of some kind. How pathetic is such talk! Instead, we need to hear the psalmist when he says, *For you have made me glad by your acts, O Lord.* Our joy may indeed arise from feelings of well-being in our human economy, but it is the creating God who is active at the heart of the matter. This way our joy becomes a gift given, a blessing received.

The psalmist adds a particularly interesting idea about people who think in this way and are open to the action of God in their lives. He says, *Those who are planted ... shall flourish ... bear fruit ... shall be green and succulent.* He seems to suggest that openness to the action of God in one's life is an ingredient for remaining fresh and creative.

Second Reading

Listen, I will tell you a mystery. Across the centuries we can almost hear the intensity and excitement in Paul's voice. He is approaching what his age would have called his peroration, the climax of a long presentation or argument. Paul knows that a great deal is riding on this. He is desperately searching for a way to put into understandable words and images the heart of Christian faith, its trust in our Lord's resurrection.

We will not all die, but we will all be changed. Paul uses the image of a great trumpet blast, something that anyone in the empire of his day would recognize as the harbinger of an important person or event that could not be ignored. What is the basis for his conviction in this vast and final transformation of human life? It is the evidence that he has looked to earlier in this great chapter. Paul has pointed to the surrounding creation, getting us to see its eternal message about death and life. The seed must die before the corn waves golden in the sun. In this miraculous transformation, this movement from life through death to transformed life, Paul sees the way for human life; and he dares to say that *this perishable body must put on imperishability.*

This same transformation, from life through death to risen life, he sees also in Jesus. This for Paul is the key piece of evidence. To the end of his days he will be conscious of the moment on the Damascus Road when he was encountered by the living presence that made itself known to him as Jesus Christ. It is on this basis that he says, *"Thanks be to God, who gives us the victory through our Lord Jesus Christ."*

But Paul is not finished. He points out the consequences that will follow from our daring to believe these things. His promise to us is nothing less than profound meaning for our lives, meaning that will never betray us. All we do in God's name is God's work. To believe this and to live this is to know that our lives are never meaningless. *In the Lord, your labour is not in vain.*

The Gospel

We can assume, I think, that this is a collection of various teachings of our Lord. They have in common a decidedly stern tone. This is not easy Christianity! It may be useful yet again to remember that scene on what Luke calls *a level place.* We do not know exactly where it was, but we do know that Jesus is facing a crowd and for some reason looks up at the newly selected disciples. The important thing is that we are the disciples! This is not a claim that we are in any way superior to the surrounding crowd; however, we are those who have accepted the responsibility that comes with Christian baptism. What we read here is directed to us!

Can a blind person guide a blind person? In repeating this old folk-saying, Jesus seems to suggest that we cannot claim to offer spiritual resources to others unless we have searched for them and found them ourselves. This is particularly true for anyone who has a ministry of preaching or teaching.

Why do you see the speck in your neighbour's eye, but do not notice the log in your own eye? We hang our heads when we read this, because we know it is the most common of human faults. Modern psychology has made us painfully aware that the *log* in our own eye is often what prompts us to focus on the *speck* in our neighbour's eye! In other words, we tend to project the shadowed parts of ourselves on to others, making them the opponent or the enemy or the personification of some evil that is in fact part of our own nature. Most of the time, we are totally unaware of what is happening. Probably because the projection of our shadow is so common in human life, and because it brings about so much damage to people and to relationships, Jesus's tone is extremely stern when he demands that we deal rigor-ously with this process in ourselves. *You hypocrite, first take the log out of your own eye.*

Jesus now digs deep into our human nature and talks about the links between our motivations and our actions. *Each tree is known by its own fruit.* No claims to virtue are to be regarded as valid or worthy when our actions belie those claims. The sure test of inner goodness is good action. Nothing else counts. Evil action points to a corresponding inner fault — *evil treas-ure* — that needs to be rooted out.

Jesus now turns to the relationship in human nature be-tween intention and action. There is a tone of exasperation when we hear him ask, *"Why do you call me 'Lord, Lord,' and do not do what I tell you?"* We can be quite sure that Jesus was very aware of this propensity in all of us, but nevertheless it makes him angry. His anger is not that of a person who wants to domi-nate and is frustrated at not being able to do so. He is con-cerned because we cannot see how a gulf between stated inten-tions and subsequent actions impoverishes our lives. Jesus is so exercised about this that he continues with a parable. Two peo-ple build two houses. One builds with deep foundations, the other with none. A flood comes. One house withstands the flood; one is swept away. It is quite obvious what makes the difference — foundations dug into rock.

The rock, as our Lord points out, is found by getting our lives together in the matter of intention and action, will and deed. To the degree that we can do this, our lives have the strength and the integrity that comes from inner consistency. Our Lord adds one more thing. If we want a basis for our lives that will be rock-like in the face of what life brings, then we will not only choose his words and his guidance, but we will act on them! Thus we become, in our Lord's words, someone who *"Comes to me, hears my words, and acts on them."*

Last Sunday after the Epiphany: The Transfiguration

Exodus 34:29–35
Psalm 99
2 Corinthians 3:12—4:2
Luke 9:28–36 (37–43)

Weavings

Being in the presence of God changes us, sometimes in ways we do not realize.

First Reading. Moses is changed as he returns from his encounter with God on the mountain. His face shines. When he becomes aware of this he hides his face.

The Psalm. As the psalmist approaches the presence of God, his awareness changes from regarding God merely as powerful to knowing God as holy.

Second Reading. For Paul, the encounter with our Lord is transforming for all who experience it.

The Gospel. On the mountain of transfiguration, not only is our Lord changed, but so are the disciples who share the experience, and so is their relationship with him.

Reflections

First Reading

Moses came down from Mount Sinai with the two tablets of the testimony in his hands. Any genuine encounter with God will leave us with a sense of having been directed towards some course of action in our lives. As we return from any such mountain-top experience, we will know that we have somehow glimpsed the law or will of God for our lives. In some sense, we will have been given a commandment, whether it be to speak, to think, to act, to make changes in our lives in some way.

The skin of [Moses'] face shone. It could not have been otherwise if he had encountered the presence of God. Our own faces shine when we have had such an experience. The sudden realization that we love or are loved. The sudden realization that we really do believe, or that we know at last what we are called to do and to be, or that we have returned from the long night of bereavement or illness. Our faces tell the tale! We have all seen this in someone else, and others have seen it in us.

Moses did not know that the skin of his face shone ... [but] ... when Aaron and all the Israelites saw Moses, the skin of his face was shining. How often in life others are aware of something about us, while to us it remains quite hidden! By the same token, we can be only too aware of something we wish to hide, and to our dismay it is perfectly obvious to others!

Notice that in this case *they were afraid to come near him [Moses].* Fear in the face of some great change can damage relationships and isolate people terribly. Illness can do this, as can bereavement. Because we have looked deep into the mysterious darkness of life, we are changed so that some others are afraid. We may have to take the initiative at such times, if we wish to help those around us to continue the relationship. *Moses called to them and [they] returned to him, and Moses spoke with them.* Notice how Moses shares his experience in full. *He gave them in commandment all that the Lord had spoken with him.*

When Moses had finished speaking with them he put a veil on his face, but whenever Moses went in before the Lord to speak with him, he took the veil off. Moses veils himself before others but unveils himself before God. So do we all, if we have a relationship with God in our lives. There is much that we try to hide from others, even — and this is ironic and rather sad — the very joy and grace that comes from a relationship with God. We conceal the very thing that would make our face shine, would we but let it! On the other hand, if we are wise, we will attempt to wear no veil in the presence of God, if only because no veil hides anything from God.

We have interpreted this passage in only one of many possible ways. St Paul interprets it in another way that we will see when we look at the epistle for today.

Psalm

Reading this psalm is like walking towards a mountain. At first it stands distant and shining, a shape, no more. A few hours later, it is possible to see certain aspects of it — a valley here, an outcrop there. By late afternoon it looms above us, yet at the same time it has become more accessible. Its relationship with us seems now more intimate. We see many things previously hidden — the scar from a long-ago rock slide, streams crossing the lower slopes, a small valley piercing into the rock face.

In the same way, the psalmist becomes aware of the infinite distance of God. *The Lord is king ... enthroned ... great in Zion ... high above all peoples.* When we view God as a far-off mountain peak, we can only be awed by the majesty of God. We become aware of our own pitiable creatureliness. Our very existence seems utterly irrelevant to that majesty.

As we continue our journey, we are given a clearer view of the nature of God. The psalmist brings his description to a climax by defining God as, above all else, *the Holy One.* It seems that the ultimate greatness is to be holy. And now, as we approach still closer to the mystery of this God, we perceive even more about God's nature. *Lover of justice ... you have executed justice.* We are being told that an essential element in being holy is to be just — not just to talk of justice but to do justice.

We make our approach still nearer to the presence of God, and we see that we are not alone. For the psalmist, there are figures of his own tradition — Moses and Aaron and Samuel. This seems to suggest that only those who are larger than life can stand in God's presence. But very quickly the psalmist cuts these people down to size. You were a God who forgave them, yet punished them for their evil deeds. The message is very clear. We don't have to run from the presence of God. Ordinary fallible humanity is welcome to stand here. That is why we can readily join the psalmist when he invites us to proclaim the greatness of the Lord.

Second Reading

This passage is painful for us to read and was probably painful for Paul to write. He is contrasting the law as a source of grace and our Lord as a source of grace. Paul is not dismissing the long centuries of the law, so much as pointing to what he has just referred to as a greater glory in Jesus Christ. For Paul, to read the old covenant is to encounter a kind of veil before one's understanding —*to this very day, when they hear the reading of the old covenant, that same veil is still there.* When Paul turns to Jesus, he finds that the veil between the human and the divine has been removed. In this new relationship there is freedom.

For a Christian, seeing Jesus is to see *the glory of the Lord as though reflected in a mirror.* Paul then gives us a glorious image. As we look into the mirror that is Jesus, we ourselves *are being transformed into the same image.*

The Gospel

A moment of shining glory and great mystery. Our Lord takes three disciples, and together they climb a nearby mountain. It may well be Mount Tabor a few miles from Nazareth. As Jesus prays, he is mysteriously changed. Within the light that blazes around him, the watchers see two great figures of their tradition, Moses and Elijah. The vision fades. The shaken Peter offers to make three shrines. As he does, a cloud hides everything. Within that shadowed moment, the disciples are addressed and pointed towards Jesus as *my Son ... my Chosen.* When they look, Jesus stands alone.

What moments of transfiguration can we ourselves claim or expect? In what direction lies our particular mountain where we may experience the presence of God? To this there is no answer, but I will attempt an insight that seems true to me. I suspect that most of us glimpse spiritual heights, not because we ourselves have climbed them but because, in the beauty and sanctity of someone's life, we have glimpsed a peak high above the lower slopes where we do most of our own journeying.

I have often thought it significant that, even though Andrew was Peter's brother, and thus was the means through whom Peter met our Lord, Andrew was not invited to see this strange radiance or to stand in the cloud. He was not on the mountain to look into the familiar face of Jesus as his brother did, to see a terrible and unfamiliar majesty shining from it.

Most of us are Andrew rather than Peter. Yet Andrew remained faithful, loyal to the community, and he went on to become one of the spiritual giants around whom the faith evolved and spread and deepened. Why? Perhaps because of what he sensed to be radiating from his brother, who after the mountain experience was the same and yet different. In some strange indefinable way, Andrew recognized that Peter had been changed by a kind of lesser transfiguration reflected from the glory of his Lord.

We discover our mountains of transfiguration in much the same way. Sometimes we find them, if it is granted to us, in a blinding moment of conversion, when we realize the presence and the utter reality of God, and we glimpse the truth and hear the call of Christ. Sometimes it is in a sacramental moment, when the bread in our hands and the wine on our lips suddenly acquire a flavour and a vintage that takes us out of time and out of our human limitations, and intoxicates us with God.

Most frequently of all, the path to our mountain of transfiguration begins in the unexpected and the ordinary: the relationship that we feel has become humdrum, until an unexpected word or gesture shines within it; the task that we resent, until a day comes when we suddenly discover a sense of vocation within it; the individual who suddenly displays an unexpected greatness or courage or faith or sweetness, who fills us with awe and before whom we almost bow down. These are the secret and unexpected, and also sacramental, openings that lead most of us to our mountains of transfiguration.